The Life and Times of Joe Gordon
(to the best of my recollection)

A Collection of Stories, Life Lessons, and Practical Jokes

by

Joseph Gordon Martin

Edited by
Ross D. Martin
and
Melissa C. Hamilton

Forward and Commentary by
Ross D. Martin

MIKE:
THANK YOU FOR YOUR
HOSPITALITY! HERE ARE
SOME OF STORIES
FROM MY FATHER YOU
MAY ENJOY...

The Life and Times of Joe Gordon
(to the best of my recollection)

© 2007 Joseph Gordon Martin

Visit www.rossmartinmd.com/joegordon.htm

for more stories, pictures and recordings.

ISBN: 1-932433-84-8

Printed by Signature Book Printing
(with thanks to Phil Nanzetta)
www.sbpbooks.com

For my "First Wife,"
Saint Sonia.
Thank you for loving me and
putting up with me
all these years.

And for my children,
Melissa and Ross,
who have given Sonia and me a few gray hairs,
a great deal of pride in their achievements,
wonderful son- and daughter-in-law,
and three terrific grandchildren.

Preface

Joseph G. Martin ("Joe Gordon") passed away on January 29th, 2009 at age 78 after battling cancer since 1989. While we are very sad about how cancer took him from us, in some ways, cancer also gave him to us for many more years. It was because of his protracted illness that Joe decided to put pen to paper and write out the stories presented in this book.

When we first published *The Life and Times of Joe Gordon (to the best of my recollection)* in 2007, we hoped that at least a few people would find enjoyment in my father's sense of humor and his special way of looking at life. None of us were prepared for the response that followed. Dad received letters, emails and calls from old friends and colleagues from across the country and abroad – some of whom he hadn't heard from in more than 50 years.

The change in my father during this time was palpable. His spirits rose; his zest for life took a real positive turn. The "Old Uncle Joe" we had all come to know and love was back in full form. It was truly a life validating experience for him and undoubtedly contributed to his beating all expectations for living beyond his predicted span.

In the end, the cancer that riddled his body had its way. But he kept his signature good humor to the very last. My sister recounts the story of when he was being wheeled into an ambulette for his final journey to a nursing home, just weeks before he passed. He was exhausted and weak and in terrible pain. At one point, his slipper fell off his foot while they rolled him to the vehicle. Once safely inside, Melissa handed him the slipper. He gazed down at it with a bewildered look, held it up to his ear, and tentatively said, "H-hello?" Ever the showman… Melissa could hardly stop laughing.

Nurses invariably would tell us of their favorite patient who, despite the pain and fatigue, always managed to offer a smile and a clever line – even when he had the energy for little else.

That's my father. His special brand of magic has been wonderfully captured in these stories. So it seemed worth doing another print run of the book. After the first printing, he continued to write out more of his favorite stories, which I'll be posting to www.rossmartinmd.com/joegordon.htm. You can also find a place to add your thoughts and stories at a memorial site: http://joe-gordon-martin.memory-of.com.

Ross D. Martin
3 February 2009

The Martin Clan and their Relationships to Joe Gordon

Back Row (left to right): Cousin Barbara Wheatcraft-Williams, Uncle Jim and Aunt Reland Gilly, Uncle Charles Gilly, Aunt Mary Gilly, Uncle Billy Gilly, Uncle Ralph Gilly *Middle Row*: Mother Glessie Gilly Martin, Uncle John and Aunt Rena Gilly (Martha Dru's Mom and Dad) *Front Row*: Cousin Barbara's Son Don Paul Williams, Cousin Martha Dru Gilly, Joe Gordon Martin

The Life and Times of Joe Gordon
(to the best of my recollection)

Table of Contents

Foreword

My father, Joseph Gordon Martin – or just "Joe Gordon" as he was universally known in his youth – had a Tom Sawyer childhood. His enchanting stories about growing up in the tiny coal mining town of Big Stone Gap, Virginia were a ready source of entertainment at social gatherings for as far back as my memory serves.

His was a colorful childhood, full of mischief and adventure, played out in the foothills of the Blue Ridge Mountains. What makes his early years even more vibrant today is the way in which he recounts each tale – as if it were a passage from a classic book rather than a distant memory. Wonderful names – like Dutchy Morris and Coach Fitchko, and places – like the Kopper Kettle and High Knob Hill, became familiar characters and magical settings in his lushly detailed stories. And without a doubt, my father knows how to tell a story.

He isn't the kind of guy who will dominate a conversation or demand attention from others. Especially as he's gotten along in years and his hearing isn't what it used to be, he never tries to take center stage. But eventually, he'll hear mention of some memory trigger and jump in with good-natured, almost boyish, enthusiasm – "Say! That reminds me of the time when…" and begin spinning a yarn that, without fail, has us all howling by the time he's finished. Then he'll go back to playing solitaire or watching TV or just listening to everyone else, the twinkle in his eye and the smile on his face fading ever so slowly.

In his stories, my father often plays the country bumpkin, the simple, hillbilly boy – never meaning any harm, but always seeming to get himself into some mix-up that quickly veers toward disaster. Just when you think he is finally going to get it, a bit of cleverness or dumb luck saves him yet again.

In reality, though, he's a very smart man and will confound many with his mastery of crosswords, Scrabble and Trivial Pursuit. He still plays the simpleton card on occasion – often for a good-natured joke. Like when someone who is too big for his polysyllabic britches pontificates, "Life is full of vicissitudes," my father might counter, "Well, I don't know about that, but it sure has its ups and downs!" – leaving the listener to do a mental double-take: is this guy really an idiot or did he know that "ups and downs" is the definition of vicissitudes? That eye twinkle is the only clue he'll give you that he's just danced a rope-a-dope around his verbal sparring partner. Whether at his own expense or his opponent's, the grins and guffaws of the witnesses are his well-earned reward.

Seems like I've heard all of his stories a thousand times, but it never seems to matter. He somehow manages to make every telling a treat. It is as though he is hauling the memory out of some old, forgotten locker for the very first time. He'll be in the middle of one of his recollections, perhaps introducing a new character. "Now what *was* that fella's name? Now, wait thar…" He'll close his eyes and rub his hands up over his forehead. "It mighta been Hanes or Holmes or– Johnny! Johnny Holmes! Yeah, that's it!" A big grin will fill his round face. Then he'll start into his highly infectious laugh and say, "Ol' Johnny was quite a character. One time when I was about twelve and he musta been fourteen…" Then he'll start off on some completely different story as if he's forgotten his place. But sure enough, he gets back to the original one, made all the better now that we know about ol' Johnny and that time when he and Dad…

Sometimes I'll just sit back and forget about trying to hear the words. Instead, I'll just listen – listen to the flow of the story as one looking through a camera with the lens out of focus. His style is one of playful excitement – rolling storylines and thoughtful pauses are interlaced with rich dialogue and punctuated with the laughter of his audience. I admire greatly his ability to weave a tale at a delicious pace – unhurried but never dragging.

If only we could find a way to preserve these wonderful stories in some fashion. In 1997, I conjured an idea for a novel that was loosely based upon Dad's youth. I started making recordings of his recollections – even traveled down to Big Stone Gap with him for his 50th high school reunion. Life got the better of my good intentions as marriage, fatherhood and career forced the project onto the shelf.

Then a few of months ago, I received a message from Dad asking me to call him at his office – not at home. He was cooking up a surprise for his "first wife, Sonia" – as he often introduces her – for their 50th wedding anniversary. He got a legal secretary he knew in Fairborn – Janet Potts – to transcribe dozens of stories he had written out longhand. (Thank you, Janet!) Would I be willing to edit them and maybe help him put them all together in a collection? You bet!

He said, "Now don't say anything about this to anybody. Janet is the only other person who knows about it. Your momma doesn't like a few of these stories, so I'm keeping it a secret for the time being. It's a whole lot of paper, so it doesn't make sense to mail them all to you since you all are heading this way in a couple of weeks anyway."

Then we started into this puzzling conversation about the logistics of me going over to Janet's office so I could read the stories there. He was making it sound as though he only had one copy of the manuscript. I asked him whether Janet used a computer or a typewriter to transcribe them. He was pretty sure it was a computer. When I suggested that Janet just email them to me, he was reluctant. I couldn't quite figure out why until he finally said he didn't want her to have to type them all over again in an email. I said my father is a very smart man; I never said he's a computer genius.

I finally convinced him that this was a good idea and that Janet wouldn't have to do any extra work. He gave me one of those "Well I'll be damned"s of his. I told him that he was about the last person on the planet who didn't have an email address. He said, "That's true, but I'm happy and I don't worry. You should have seen your mother when her computer died and she lost all her stuff. That never happens to me."

So maybe my father *is* a computer genius.

Computer genius or not, Dad sure knows how to tell a story. I was amazed at how well they read on paper. Still, there was a decent amount of editing required and I'm indebted to my sister, Missy Martin – now Melissa Hamilton, for helping out with some of the work. But it was mostly just getting the quote marks in the right places and filling in some blanks. The essence and pace of the stories were all there and in great form.

I added some final polish to this collection by sorting these random snapshots in a roughly chronological order and grouping them into sections that reflect the major chapters of Dad's rich and colorful life. To provide a little context, I've added some brief commentary at the beginning of each chapter. The stories, though, stand on their own and can be read in most any order.

Thank you, Dad, for making this magical thing. I look forward to the day when your grandson, Taylor, is old enough to enjoy these stories (for a few of them, he will need to be at least 18!). It is a great and precious gift.

Enough with the introductions and on with the tales, which my father swears are all true – to the best of his recollection...

Ross D. Martin

January 1, 2007

Part 1
Growing Up in Big Stone Gap

The Early Years

Joseph Gordon Martin was born on the third floor of The Touraine, an apartment building in Big Stone Gap, on September 17th, 1930 to Joseph Alfred and Glessie Lipps Martin. Named after the French province, The Touraine was built as a hotel in 1905. That building served as the main stage for Dad's life in Big Stone Gap.

Glessie managed the 14 apartments beginning in 1934. About all she was paid at first was rent-free living, for which the family was grateful as the Great Depression was being felt by almost everyone. According to his Aunt Mary, Dad was raised on little more than beans and cornbread; Glessie sacrificed just to pay for his milk.

While his childhood may have been lacking in material wealth, it was rich in the things that really matter in a child's life – family, friends... and adventure!

A Call to Santa

Do you believe in Santa Claus? Your answer really doesn't make any difference because *I do*.

When I was about five years old, Jimmy Gilley told me there was no Santa Claus. Jimmy was about 12 and older brother to my friend Kenny. "It's your mom and dad," he stated with authority. "They get up early in the morning and leave stuff around the tree."

I thought about it for a while and then remembered my first toy train I had gotten for Christmas. It was not electric and had been hastily set up. And the cars were not in order like the picture on the box! Maybe Jimmy Gilley was right.

So I stomped into the living room at my house and declared, "There is no Santa Claus!" Dad was reading the paper and Mom was reading her book. Dad never put down the paper but Mom asked, "Who said that?"

"Jimmy Gilley!" I answered defiantly. "He said it's you and Daddy."

My father pulled the paper up higher. I can't recall if it was shaking because of hidden laughter, but Mom, always calm, said, "Why don't you try calling him?"

"You mean at the *North Pole*?"

"Since you don't believe in him, you might just see if he really exists."

Trembling, I picked up the phone. Miss Georgia Cox, our night operator, came on the line. "Miss Georgia, I want to call the North Pole!" I said matter-of-factly.

"Is that you, Joe Gordon?" asked Miss Georgia.

"Yes, ma'am, and I want to talk to Santa," as if she needed to know.

"Well, Joe Gordon, the North Pole is a long way off so it might take me a little while but you stay right there and I'll get him for you."

Mom went back to reading her book and Dad continued with his paper. I can't recall if he turned a page. I sat with my arms crossed, waiting.

Then the phone rang. Mom said she wished she had had a camera to record the expression on my face. "Aren't you going to answer it?"

Slowly I picked up the phone. "H-H-Hullo?"

A booming base voice said, "Is this Joe Gordon Martin?"

Barely able to talk and with a trembling voice, I said, "Y-Y-Yes, sir."

Again the big voice said, "I understand that you don't believe in me."

"I do! I do!" I frantically proclaimed.

Then the voice softened. "I know you have been a good boy so I'm coming to see you."

I sat there stunned. I think Mom asked me about what he had said. I don't think I replied. Instead I jumped up and ran over to Jimmy's house and yelled out, "There *is* a Santa Claus." Then I hauled off and hit him as hard as I could in the stomach. He recoiled and knocked the hell out of me. I went home crying, but I still believed in Santa Claus.

Years later – I was 18 – I went to Kelly Chevrolet to purchase my first car – a '54 Bellaire Coupe. A salesman, Raymond Horne, asked, "Tell me, Joe Gordon, do you still believe in Santa Claus?"

"It was you!" I cried out.

"Yes, it was me," he said. "I got a call from Miss Georgia – 'Joe Gordon Martin doesn't believe in Santa Claus and wants to call the North Pole and speak to Santa. You have a nice low voice. Will you talk to him?' 'What will I say?' I asked. She says, 'Just tell him that he's a good boy and you're coming to see him.' And so I did."

As I said before, I *still* believe in Santa Claus.

Boy Winos

Paul McConnell and I went fishing in the Powell River in Big Stone Gap. Our regular fishing hole was being used that day by a big black man.

We noticed that often he would lay down his bamboo pole and take a bottle he had stowed in the bushes. He would take a healthy swig, screw the top on and carefully put it back into the bushes.

After a while he gathered up his pole, worm can, and a couple of small fish and climbed up the embankment. Pretty soon he was out of sight.

Paul and I waded across the river to see what he had been drinking. Turned out it was blackberry wine. I was about nine at the time and Paul was one year older. The bottle was about half full.

"Let's drink it!" Paul said.

"Okay!" I replied.

Paul carefully wiped off the mouth of the bottle with his sleeve. We didn't want to catch any germs! He then took a great big drink. After he got that down he exclaimed, "Wow!"

I grabbed the bottle and tried to emulate Paul. I didn't go WOW! I gasped and hacked.

Paul took the bottle away from me and tilted it high for another large drink.

"Hoo-wee!" he yelled out. I thought I would try it again to find out if it was going to taste like it did before. So I took a big swig. I hacked and tried to clear my throat – the same reaction as the first time. Paul finished it off.

We gathered up our stuff and went to Paul's house, which was nearby. Immediately, Paul's mother suspected something. I guessed it was because we were acting silly, but it was really because of her keen sense of smell.

"Paul, come over here!" she demanded. She smelled his breath. "What have you boys been drinking? It smells like wine!" We started giggling again. "Let me smell your breath, Joe Gordon!" I obeyed. It confirmed her suspicion.

"I can't let you go home like that, Joe Gordon," she said. "Your mother will whale the tar out of you! I'll call her and ask her if you can eat supper with us and spend the night." Mom said okay.

Thank goodness Paul's father was out of town. As far as I know, she never told anyone about us two young winos!

Uncle Charles

Every boy or girl should have an uncle like my Uncle Charles. Successful businessman, stunt pilot, inventor – he was generous and rich. I'll share a story that will give you some idea what he was like: my first visit to Cincinnati...

Uncle Charles had invited me to spend a week with him and said I could bring a friend. At that time, Paul McConnell was my best friend. I was 12 and he a year older. Mom paid for my round trip train ticket and gave me a few dollars spending money. Paul's parents had done basically the same, except Paul had a few bucks more because he worked after school for Kroger as a bag and stock boy.

We left the station at 11:00 a.m. at a place we called the "L&N" for Louisville and Nashville. The name came from the fact that the L&N railroad was the only rail line to get out of Big Stone Gap via the southern route. The north part of Big Stone also had a train depot called "The Southern." Southern Railroad served the coalfields and the passengers who needed to go north for connections elsewhere.

The L&N higher ups did not like it one bit that they were mandated to have a passenger car and a mail car attached to the coal train. But rules were rules. So, to comply with the federal directive, they had a passenger car that I know must have been around since the 1900s. It had straight-back wicker seats (if they could be set at an angle, I couldn't figure out how), windows that opened (including several that couldn't close), gaslights that hung down from the ceiling, and a potbelly coal stove at one end. On account of WWII being on and all, the officials at L&N declared they were providing the best they could but that the better cars were being assigned to their main lines.

Once on board, Paul and I dashed to a seat that had an open window. When the train went through a mountain pass and the wind was just right, cinders would blow back into the car. It didn't take too long for us to discover this, so we found seats where the window was closed. This was not hard to do because so few people were aboard. Thus we began our journey.

We were surprised to find we would go a few miles and then stop at a "nowhere" place. Maybe we could see a house or two, but that was it. The conductor told us that sometimes it was a mail stop and sometimes they had to let people on or off. This is why I think some came to call it the TP&W railroad – "Take Pains and Walk!"

The train got to Corbin, Kentucky about four in the afternoon. From there we caught the Orange Blossom Special coming up from Florida. What a contrast! Although crowded with passengers, it hurtled nonstop to Cincinnati.

Uncle Charles was to meet us upon our arrival that evening at ten. We made it right on schedule. He did write, however, that if he wasn't there, we were to take a taxi to the hotel. We lugged my very heavy bag to the front of the station. Mother had packed as if I was going to be gone for a couple of months. Our passenger car was at the very end of the track. It was awfully hard for me to carry the bag because of my skinny physique.

Getting off the car, I looked up the platform. A very long way off were the steps leading to the main terminal. Just then a red cap appeared, "Take yo' bags, suh?" he cheerfully asked as he picked up my bag. Quickly Paul told him to set the bag down and that I could take care of it myself. "Yes, suh!" And he just as cheerfully obliged.

"Why did ya' do that?" I demanded.

"You don't know how much he would have charged you to carry that, do ya'?" he retorted. "He coulda' charged you a dollar – maybe two – and you couldn't do nuthin' about it! My Daddy told me you gotta watch these people."

What could I say – the red cap had disappeared to look for other, more prosperous prospects.

I struggled to get the bag to the outside of the terminal. Vainly I looked for Uncle Charles. It was way past ten o'clock so I said, "Maybe we should take a taxi to the hotel."

Paul was having none of that idea. "Daddy told me to specifically watch out for cab drivers. You don't know the town. Daddy said they can run you around and charge you a lot of money and you wouldn't know the difference."

The front of the station was crowded with travelers coming and going. So, Paul asked a distinguished looking gentleman if he could help us. "What was the name of the hotel, Joe?" he asked. I took a piece of paper from my pocket where Mom had written "Netherland Plaza Hotel."

The man said, "Oh yes. Do you see that big tall building?" pointing to downtown Cincinnati.

"Yes, sir," Paul replied.

"Well," said the gentleman, "that is the Carew Tower and the Netherland Plaza Hotel is in that tower."

"Thanks!" said Paul. And with that, he picked up his bag and started to go.

"Where ya' goin'?" I asked.

"We're gonna walk to the hotel," he stated as a matter of fact.

The man interjected. "Boys," he said, "it must be at least two miles from here to the hotel."

With that knowledge, I put my bag down and told Paul, "I'm gonna take a taxi whether you come or not. I'm not gonna walk that far with this heavy bag."

Paul could see I meant business. A taxi was waiting right beside us. I put my bag on the back seat and sat down beside it. Reluctantly – and I mean reluctantly – Paul got in. "Where to?" the driver asked and I told him the Netherland Plaza.

The cabbie let his foot off the clutch and the taxi started rolling. He then reached across the seat and pulled the flag down on the meter. Immediately 35 cents appeared on the meter.

The back door flew open and out jumped Paul!

The driver slammed on the breaks. Paul yelled at me from outside the car. "We ain't gone ten feet and he's charging 35 cents already!"

The driver tried to allay Paul's fears by saying, "Look fellas, it's not going to cost you over a buck to get you to the hotel."

Still standing on the curb, Paul asked the man who gave us directions to verify what the taxi driver said. "One dollar and no more." The cab driver just shook his head.

Upon our arrival the bellhops, the desk clerks, elevator operator – seems like everybody – breathed with relief that we had safely arrived. Evidently, the manager at the hotel had been instructed to take good care of us.

Since Uncle Charles lived at the hotel, I asked for his room. Without calling, the desk clerk said he was still out for the evening; however, he would inform him that we were there and in bed.

The next morning we stopped by the front desk to see if there was any message. The clerk handed me an envelope – in it was a note and a $20 bill. The note was from Uncle Charles saying that he would see us for dinner about six that evening and, as a suggestion, we might want to take a steamboat – the *Island Queen* – to Coney Island, an amusement park.

This sounded good to us. So off we went to explore the great city of Cincinnati!

The first thing we did was we got lost. This was one trait of Paul's that I didn't like. Since he was older and much bigger than me, he felt he had the right to lead. After the second time we got lost, I put my foot down. "Next time we're gonna ask directions," I said in my no-nonsense voice.

"Awright! Awright!" he replied. From then on we didn't get lost.

What fun! Coney Island had roller coasters and rides of all kinds. But our favorite was the bumper cars. For thrills we preferred the roller coasters, but for all around fun it was the bumper cars for sure. The roller coasters cost 25 cents and the bumper cars only a dime. I can't remember the cost of a round trip aboard the *Island Queen*, but I do remember we had money left over – even after stuffing ourselves with Coney Island hot dogs, double hamburgers, and gallons of Coca-Cola.

Every day for five days we did the same routine and we still weren't bored. I saw Uncle Charles three times in all – once at dinner the day after we got there, one night at Coney Island for supper, and a third time when he took me shopping at an exclusive men's store in Cincinnati. There he bought me a pair of penny loafers, my first. I wore them until they fell apart.

Funny thing: at Coney Island, an attractive waitress spotted him and said in a very sultry voice, "Hi, Gilly! Whatcha doing here?"

"I'm taking my nephew and his friend to dinner."

"I get off at ten, or maybe I can make it earlier," she cooed.

"Thanks." (He couldn't remember her name!) "Uh-uh. I promised the boys I would take them to a movie."

Upon our departure he had his secretary take us to the train station and see us off. At supper, the second night we were there, he had admonished us to tell our parents that he was with us every single day. We weren't about to tell our parents anything to the contrary!

Uncle Jim and Aunt Reland

Mom was the oldest of the Gilly clan; James Tilden was one of its members. He married Reland Tate from the Cracker's Neck section of Powell Valley, Virginia. You might call it a small village. The two-lane highway ended at Skeen's General Store. Two gravel roads branched off from there.

Aunt Reland worked at Uncle John's drug store, mostly behind the long soda fountain. But her main job was preparing food for the lunch crowd. She prepared mostly sandwiches – which were delicious – and she also made pies. My mouth still waters when I think about her lemon pie! Made from scratch, it was not firm like the store-bought ones, but kind of spread out when cut and served. At family dinners, she would bake her famous Parker House rolls. She had to make a lot of them. When you slathered them with home-churned butter, they melted in your mouth.

Uncle Jim was the bookish type. Not given to quick witty retorts, he seemed to think things through before the response. He was always neatly dressed with starched collars, pressed suits, and shined shoes. Naturally, he worked in the accounting department for Interstate Railroad. Interstate was one unusual railroad. They only had, I believe, 300 miles of rail track, but they had many, many coal cars. The L&N and Southern Railways hauled the coal-laden cars from the large yard out into the world. The locomotives around the Interstate were called "switch" engines and they were used to place the coal cars in line for pick-up.

Uncle Jim gave me one of the most exciting gifts a boy approaching his teens could have… a ride in the cab of a steam engine! On a Saturday morning, he and I went to Appalachia where the railroad yards were. He had to give me a boost to get me into the cab of the monster of iron. The engineer asked me if I wanted to drive the train. This I hadn't expected! "Yes, sir!" I quickly answered, although I was scared half to death.

The engineer stood me on his seat next to the window. "All right – everything is clear, let's go!" he said. Placing my hand on the throttle he said, "Pull hard!" I pulled with all my might!

The engine started to move. Only the coal tender was attached so we were not pulling a heavy load. A loud Chug! Then vibration – another chug! A third chug and we started picking up speed. The noise was loud, but not as loud as my beating heart! "Better blow the whistle so folks can know we're a-comin'!" Cautiously I pulled the cord. A low whistle sounded. "Pull it down more!" he yelled over the noise. What a sound!

I don't know how long I performed as an engineer – probably five minutes or so. We attached loaded coal cars (by then the engineer was back at the controls). The morning passed so quickly!

Around this time of my life, on most days after school and on some Saturdays I would help "Gene" who owned a shoe store next to my Uncle John's drug store. He wouldn't let me sell, but he needed help with counting the inventory, keeping the shoeboxes in order and that sort of thing.

After school one day I went to his store as usual only to find it closed. I went next door to find Uncle John who told me that Gene had been arrested and had spent the night in jail! I couldn't believe it! The following day I literally ran to his store after school when I heard he had been released while awaiting his trial date.

Gene was raving about how unjustly he had been treated by our Chief of Police, Barron Lane. He maintained that he had been arrested after having just a "few" beers. Uncle Jim was at my house when I came home. I was still steamed up as I related Gene's story.

Uncle Jim, as I said, was a thinker. He casually asked me, "Did you hear the other side of the story?" I admitted I had not, but I knew of Chief Lane's reputation as a brute. I had no reason to doubt Gene's story.

Uncle Jim suggested we go and talk to "Stony" Thompson, the owner of the poolroom where the incident took place. Stony said he had witnessed the whole thing. Gene had come staggering into the bar, demanding a beer.

"I tried to calm Gene down, but he was all fired up about something! He was yelling and cursing so we called the police. When Barron Lane got here, Gene became more belligerent and tried to fight Barron. You know Barron is much bigger than Gene, so there was not much of a fight to it. Since Gene wouldn't settle down Barron hauled him off to jail to cool him down.

Even after hearing the "other side" of the story, I still was having a hard time conceiving of Gene being drunk and picking a fight with Chief Lane.

The following day I went to Gene's store. Gene was still raving about the arrest. It was then that I smelled the liquor on his breath. He was slurring his words and I realized he must be drunk. In the back storage room I found the remains of a bottle of whiskey.

I quit going to his store. Not too long after that, the store closed and I heard Gene had been sent off to an alcoholic rehab center. I never saw him after that.

I did go to my Uncle Jim and apologize for my anger upon hearing Gene's side of the story. Uncle Jim affirmed that there are two sides to every story. Only with facts can you determine whom to believe.

Uncle Billy

All my life, Uncle Billy had lived with us in *The Touraine*. He had to leave school in the sixth grade because it was determined he was incapable of learning more at the next level.

I never knew how to classify Uncle Billy's mental state. Moron? Imbecile? He could read a little – especially the Bible and could even quote a few lines from it. Mom paid him a little money to keep the coal-fired furnaces going in the apartment house, even though she employed a janitor. He had menial jobs like dishwashing at Martin Alvis' Café, or sweeping offices – that sort of thing.

He had his teeth pulled because he loved sugary products and did not take care of his teeth. He had been fitted for dentures, but refused to wear them because they hurt his mouth. He did not talk plainly in the first place and without his dentures it was even harder to understand him.

He hated noise and when other kids would come to my house he would inevitably come into the room demanding that we quiet down. Naturally, this would embarrass me to no end.

Actually, he was a sweet guy – at least until he and his friends, the town drunks, would get sauced on cheap wine. Then he would turn into somebody else. He would come into Mom's bedroom with a "Nobody loves me" attitude and proceeded to lay out all his grievances, his hurts – anything that was bottled up inside him.

Several times I would wake up hearing these ravings and would go running into Mom's bedroom to see that he didn't become violent. He cursed and flailed his arms but never struck Mom or me.

Mom would quietly listen and after a while would say something like, "You are right, Billy. Let's talk about it some more tomorrow. We both need some sleep." Usually he would stagger off to bed. I think he just needed someone to listen to him.

One night I was entertaining a group of friends. Uncle Billy came home and had evidently been drinking. He starts off mumbling "Too much noise," and other grievances hardly understandable. My friends quietly left.

I had had enough! The next morning, I confronted my mother. "Mom!" I said in a demanding voice. "Why does Uncle Billy have to live with us? Why can't he live with Uncle John or Uncle Jim? They can take him in!"

Mom looked me directly in the eye and said in a very matter-of-fact voice. "Uncle Billy cannot help what he is. *You* can help what you are. He can't change, but you can. He will live with us as long as he is able and I will take care of him."

I was an only child. On that day I learned that the world did not revolve around me. The sooner I learned that fact – and learned to live with it – the happier I would be. How true! How true!

My First Strip Show

Gary Collier and I had thumbed a ride to Appalachia to see a carnival. At that time Gary was about 14 and I a year younger. Walking around the grounds, we stopped at a sideshow. The barker was describing the excitement of an exotic dancer. "She wiggles! She bumps! She grinds! And she will cause your eyes to pop right out of their sockets!"

The word "exotic" was enough to interest Gary and me into seeing the show. Inside the tent, up in front of us was a rickety looking dance platform. No seats; standing room only. When Gary and I worked our way to the stage, it was about Gary's eye level. I was about two inches taller than Gary.

Pretty soon the front tent flaps were closed and the afternoon sun beating down on the canvas gave everything a kind of an orange glow. The barker bounded onto the stage and extolled the audience to give a warm welcome to the "little lady." Gary and I dared not to turn around for fear we might miss something in front of us. The barker started the music, which was a very old phonograph and a much used record on the turntable.

"Now, ladies and gentlemen," he announced, "we'll begin the spectacular show!"

I quickly glanced around. I didn't see any ladies. I also didn't see any men you would characterize as gentlemen. The music started with emphasis on the drum: Kaboom - Kaboom. Then she appeared.

Heavily made up, she looked to be about 40-ish, best as I could tell. I'll never forget the silky red outfit with black trim, a long black boa, and wide-mesh stockings with gaping holes in them. I don't know how long she danced; mostly she just sashayed around the dance floor and did a few bumps and grinds. Then the music stopped. The dancer quickly disappeared behind a canvas curtain. The barker came out. "Now ladies and gentlemen, you're going to see a real show. We couldn't talk about it on the outside because it's a little bit risqué, but for only the price of a half a dollar – a single 50-cent piece or two small quarters – the little lady will put on a show that you will never forget!"

Unfortunately, I didn't have a half a dollar. Gary only had a quarter. Gary asked the M.C. if he put one hand over one eye could he see the show for 25 cents. "Go away, kid. You're too young for this kind of a show anyway!"

As Gary and I turned to leave a voice from the rear of the crowd said, "I'll take care of them boys." It was Mr. Quessenbury, a builder from Big Stone Gap – and a friend of my mother's! Oh, Lord! With that he came forward with three half dollars.

The music started and once again the "little lady" came out. She turned her back to the audience and us. Suddenly, she turned around and looking Gary straight in the eye said, "Now you boys are going to get you an eyeful!"

With that she pulled out a water pistol and shot Gary squarely between the eyes. She took aim at me but I was able to duck before she ran out of water in the gun. The audience erupted with laughter.

For years after that, whenever I walked down the streets in Big Stone Gap with my mother and Mr. Quessenbury saw us, he would start laughing. "Mr. Quessenbury must think you are very funny!" she'd say.

"Yeah, Mom we've had a lot of laughs."

The Ghost of Marse Collier

This is a totally politically incorrect story of a practical joke I was involved with in my early teens.

Frank Laws was a young black boy about ten years old. His mother, a wonderful lady, worked for Mrs. Anna Barron Morris. Anna Barron's house was a stately two story home atop a hill with an "L" shaped front porch. It was built by Mrs. Morris' Grandfather, Mr. Collier or "Marse" Collier, as the black folk called him.

One day, several of us young teenagers and Frank Law were sitting around in what I guess you'd call the family room because the front room and the dining room were strictly "off limits" to us. The Morris family (for the purpose of this story) consisted of three boys, John Ed, a senior in High School, Dutchy, a year older than me, and Bob, a year younger than me. I'm trying to recall just who was there that afternoon. I believe it was Bob, Bill Wolfe, Gene Collier, Frank Laws and me.

Frank Laws brought up the subject of Marse Collier. He told us that some of his family had told him that the ghost of Marse Collier haunted the house and every once in a while he would appear. My mind quickly started working. I asked Bob, "Isn't this the night that your great granddaddy's ghost will appear?"

Bob took it from there. "Yeah, as a matter of fact, tonight *is* the night he's supposed to appear," he said. "Frank! Do you want to see him?"

"I don't want see no ghost!" Frank loudly exclaimed.

Attempting to allay his fears, Bob said, "Frank, we'll all be with you so you don't have to be afraid."

"I dunno…"

"We'll hide in the basement behind the furnace so he won't see us," Bob explained. "He won't hurt us." Bob added. It was evident that Frank wanted some kind of assurance that we would be in the basement with him and that we would find safety in numbers. Reluctantly, Frank agreed.

Then we got to work. First, I suggested we get a sheet and cut two eye holes in it to put over me. That was important for a ghost imitator. But, we needed something else – something to make the ghost appear to be an apparition.

Bob came up with a perfect solution. He found a wood estimator's measuring stick. At one end was a flat metal stop or lip that would keep the stick from moving towards you as you pulled it against some lumber. The handle was like a trowel's pear-shaped handle, but hand-size. The length was a little longer than a yardstick and it too was made of wood. When I held it out at arm's length it was about 5 feet from my body. We set a candle on the end next to the metal stop. Since the device was heavy, when I held it with my outstretched arm, it would gently move up and down about five or six inches. Then Bob came up with a thick, heavy logging chain. Perfect!

The basement was poured concrete – including the steps – and about 40 feet long, stopping at the coal bin. Naturally, the furnace was at that end. On the left side was an eight-foot workbench and across the room was another room they called a canning room with shelves on three sides.

On the workbench sat a kid's Morse code sender and receiver. You could send the code with a dot-dash click or by a small light bulb that would come on when you pressed the key. Perfect! Next, we got hold of a small skull model of a human head. Experimenting, we discovered that, when you put the Morse code receiver into the skull, it lit up the eyes. The faint light gave an eerie look to the skull in the dark. We placed this skull on the top shelf of the canning room, next to the ceiling, as far back as we could. With the lights out, it looked really scary when we pressed the sender key. We placed the sender on the workbench.

We had rehearsed over and over the appearance of Marse Collier. With the lights out, the candle gave an eerie glow to the sheet, and dragging the heavy chain down the steps made a perfect rattle. Now we had to wait for nightfall and for Frank to show up. Thank goodness Mrs. Morris was attending a meeting and John Ed – her oldest son – we didn't know his schedule.

Everything was in place. Bob told Frank that I would not be there but Bill and Gene would be. Bob went with Frank and they crouched down beside the furnace. I can't remember where Gene hid but Bill was to turn off the basement lights and then hide.

In my best ghostly voice I painfully called out slowly, "Frank, where are you?" Then I would take a step – rattle, rattle, rattle. "Frank… Frank… I'm coming to see you, Frank…" I felt a breeze go by me.

Then I heard a loud voice yell out, "Frank what the hell are you doing? Get out from under the couch!"

John Ed was home!

Bob called out, "Where'd Frank go?" Bill turned on the lights… No Frank. I quickly stashed my costume and equipment under the workbench and ran up the stairs with the others into the family room. There was Frank – half under the upturned couch with John Ed tugging at his legs trying to pull him out.

"I seen him! I seen him!" yelled Frank, crying and trembling.

"Seen who?" John Ed asked in a calming voice.

"I seen the ghost of Marse Collier!" Frank cried out. "I seen him! I seen him!"

Instantly, John Ed knew the problem with Frank – and he was *angry*! "What the hell are you doing scaring Frank like that?" Then he turned to Frank and soothingly said, "There's no ghost. It's these boys playing like there's a ghost." John Ed figured out we must have created the scene in the basement so he takes Frank by the hand and said, "Come on Frank. I'll show you. There's no ghost of Marse Collier." With that everyone proceeded to the basement.

It couldn't have worked out better. The door to the canning room was closed. John Ed told Frank to open it to see that there was no ghost there. John Ed had his back turned away from the door while Frank cautiously looked in. Then Bob pressed the key that lit the light in the skull. Frank screamed and went up the stairs like lightning. That was the same breeze that had passed me earlier!

Once again John Ed chased after Frank and once again Frank sought cover underneath the couch and once again there was John Ed pulling Frank's legs trying to dislodge him from the couch. Now John Ed was really mad. "I don't know what you're doing to scare this boy half to death but I'm telling you to knock it off." With that he ordered all the "ghosts" to immediately leave the house.

Now, I know *I* don't believe in the ghost of Marse Collier, but I can't vouch for Frank.

My Mom — Glessie L. Martin

Glessie Lipps Gilly Martin was one of eight children born to Gordon E. and Elizabeth Gilly. She left us in 1977 at the age of 84 after succumbing to cancer.

Dad's father, Joseph Alfred Martin, didn't play as prominent a role in Dad's life as did his Mother. His pursuit of gainful employment during hard times often kept him far from home. He died suddenly when Dad was only sixteen.

The Martin Family fortunes began to change as Glessie found that she had a penchant for real estate – a gift she apparently passed on to her son as time would eventually tell. She eventually bought The Touraine – the apartment building where she raised Dad – and many other local properties.

Even though Big Stone Gap didn't have many things to do for a kid from the 'burbs like me, I always looked forward to making the long, winding drive from Ohio to Virginia to see Grandma Martin and Aunt Mary at The Touraine. My favorite part of our family visits was getting to play a schoolboy as an extra in Big Stone's one true attraction – the summer outdoor drama The Trail of the Lonesome Pine. For years, Grandma Martin played the role of Ole Hon, a clay pipe-smoking mountain woman with a wise but gentle gaze and good advice. That's pretty much what she was like in real life – minus the clay pipe.

Glessie was a true Southern Gentlewoman. Even in my youth, I sensed that she was a person of great wisdom and regal bearing; it was easy to see why my father held her in such high esteem. These stories capture just a glimpse of her wonderful character.

Postmaster Martin

I cannot tell stories about my own life unless I talk about Mom, Glessie Lipps Gilly Martin. An unusual name, you might say. And I would agree. My grandfather, Gordon Early Gilly had an interesting name also. He was named by his father, John Barger Gilly who fought for the Confederacy under Generals Gordon and Early, hence his name.

As I understand it, my grandfather found the name Glessie in a novel in which she was the heroine. The "Lipps" came from another branch of the Gilly clan. Note the spelling "Gilly." Most times it's spelled "Gilley." Evidently, some years before my grandfather came along, there was a split in the family – some stayed with one spelling; my side dropped the extra letter.

I'll digress for a moment. Years ago I was an Emcee at a banquet. The main speaker was an Englishman. While we chatted before his speech, he mentioned that he studied the derivation of English names as a hobby.

He said "Martin – that's pretty much Welsh and Scottish." I replied that I was aware of that but on my mother's side of the family we're Gilly's!"

"Gilly – oh, yes, yes!" he gleefully replied. "It means country bumpkin!"

Having traveled to England, Scotland, and Ireland, I now know better. Long ago, a "gilly" was a gamekeeper for an estate. Not a bad job in those days.

While we're on the subject of name calling, my great, great grandfather was George Washington Gilley. As you can probably guess, his father was in the Revolutionary War. I have never been able to verify this, but this is what Mom was told by her grandfather.

My father ran a Shell filling station and did a limited amount of repair work on automobiles. Prior to that, my dad had a job with the Work Projects Administration (WPA). The work was hard and the hours long. Dad's work day started at six in the morning, so we were up around 4:30 am. Dad had no car and had to depend upon someone picking him up, so he was out early to wait for a ride to work. I can recall protesting to Mom that I didn't have to get up that early because I didn't work. Mom would have none of that. Families shared the breakfast and evening meals together as a family and that was that.

Mom was a good writer. She wrote for Carl Knight's weekly newspaper, *The Big Stone Gap Post*. The pay was small, but it was work that she enjoyed. It gave her an opportunity to write a column, which she called "Just Odds and Ends." The townsfolk loved her stories and observations; years later when visiting home, the old timers told me how much they enjoyed her column.

In 1945 the Civil Service Commission began selecting postmasters by examination. Heretofore the position had been a political plum of a job for those who served the party well. Mom decided she would take the test and apply for the job. After all, my grandfather, great grandfather and great, great uncle had all been postmasters in Big Stone Gap. As a matter of fact, great, great uncle Elkhanna Gilley had been the first!

But it was not family tradition that drove her. She really believed a woman could do a postmasters job just as well as a man. This was a rare opportunity to prove the point.

The Democratic Party had been in power for quite some time and the current Postmaster, James R. Taylor, had served in the position for just over two years. He had succeeded his brother, Isaac Taylor, after he died.

Mom took the test and made the highest score. Jim Taylor also took the test but didn't do as well. Naturally, this upset the party officials who were sure that Jim would be heir apparent. Somehow or other they were able to have the test thrown out.

Another test was scheduled; again my mother had the high score. I'll never forget the day the party leaders called upon Mom. They met in our living room and I sat there in awe. These were business leaders and highly respected members of Wise County – a veritable Who's Who among the local folk.

They approached the subject very carefully explaining to Mom that historically this has been a "man's" job. As head of a household, he would provide for his family whereas Mom was not the sole provider for the family since, ironically, my father was a clerk at the post office at the time.

They also appealed to her sense of loyalty to the party. Jim and his brother had been pillars of the community and great supporters of the party.

I remember Mom patiently listening to these gentlemen. And in her quiet response she thanked them for taking the time to come to see her. Then she gave a very terse reply, saying she had no intention of giving up the job.

Naturally, the spokesmen for the party in a veiled threat said there probably would be another test. This infuriated Mom. That night she carefully composed a letter to Senator Robinson of Virginia telling him that if she had to take another test she would go all the way to Washington to call upon the Civil Service Commission.

In less than two weeks, Senator Robinson wrote Mom that assured her there would not be a third test.

On May 8, 1945, Glessie L. Martin was officially sworn in as Postmaster of Big Stone Gap, Virginia – a happy day for the Martin household!

But Mom was a bit troubled. As I mentioned before, my father worked at the post office at the time. He would have to give up his position because nepotism was not allowed. So Dad went to work at a state run liquor store in Abington. He was a very quiet man and, when he came home on weekends, he seemed happy. Two years later, he died of a massive cerebral hemorrhage. I was sixteen.

After Mom became Postmaster, our world changed. Seems Mother had another latent talent that we were not aware of: the ability to make money in real estate.

It all started with her purchase of the Wentz house. Ted Wentz had been the owner of a coal company. One day he went hunting in the mountains. For reasons that remain a mystery, he didn't take his two beloved hunting dogs. His body was found a few days later. He had been shot to death. That's all I recall of the incident; to my knowledge the killer was never found.

The house was occupied for several years after Wentz's death; when those folks moved out, the property remained vacant for a long time.

The heirs to the property lived in Richmond, Virginia. They had somehow remembered Mom and called her. Did she know of anyone who might like a large home in a very nice area?

Mom said she would look into it. The Victorian style mansion had a parlor, living room, solarium, and huge dining room. On the second floor were six bedrooms and three full baths. A half bath was on the first floor. The master bedroom went across the second story. At one end was a turret (a circular room) – a great place for reading books. The high huge kitchen had a butler's pantry. The one-story carriage house held two carriages and the maid's quarters were in the rear. To top it off, the mansion was located on Popular Hill – "Where da rich folks lived!"

The lady in Richmond told Mom she would sell the property for $8,000! Mom said that was a reasonable price and agreed to buy it at that price. Brownie Polly, superintendent of mining operations in Derby, VA, had heard the property was for sale before Mom did and could have purchased it then for $8,000. He turned it down. Two months later, Stonega Coal and Coke Company told Mr. Polly he had to relocate to Big Stone. Mom sold the house to him for $10,000! I don't know if he ever got over that transaction. He and his wife spent a lot of money repairing and decorating and it turned out to be a lovely home.

An Interstate Highway Comes through Big Stone

Mr. Coots (I hope I spelled his name right) was a plumber. Originally, he hailed from Scotland but never lost his brogue. I must have been six or seven years old when he would come to talk with Mom at our apartment.

He wore bib overalls, a crisply starched white dress shirt, a small, black bow tie, and a man's hat. The reason he came to see Mom was he had a particular obsession: he was convinced that U.S. Highway 23 should become this major North-South route in the USA. US 23 ran through Big Stone and he could visualize our town becoming a major tourist attraction.

Since he was a bachelor and lived in a small room behind his shop he found time to write voluminous tomes to the U.S. Department of Commerce. He used an old Underwood typewriter and several of the typebars would stick together. As a result, the words were often hard to read. He was not a very educated man, mostly self taught in his trade.

He would telephone Mom for an appointment to see her. Upon his arrival, he would reach in his pocket and pull out a brand new, bright penny for me. I really felt important. Upon seeing Mom he would doff his hat make a bow. After exchanging pleasantries, he would go into an old battered brief case and take out his latest letter to the Department of Commerce.

He would then sit patiently while Mom read the letter. Invariably she would ask for time to review his writing and make her comments on the margin. Thanking her over and over again, he would bow and leave.

Even though he was not a good writer, his rationale made good sense. Mother liked Mr. Coots and, being civic-minded herself, she encouraged his dream. The possibility of this happening became more remote when US-25 through Kentucky was widened and became the route of choice for Michiganders and Ohioans going to Florida. Later, I-75 was built along the route of US-25.

Mr. Coots died at a ripe old age without seeing his dream fulfilled.

Years later, after becoming the town Postmaster, Mom heard that a major highway was coming through BSG sometime in the future. Mom thought the future was now.

Don Wax worked at the post office. He was best described as an entrepreneur with many talents. Investing in property was one; writing came in second. Mom liked Don very much and would tell me about Don's latest adventures into the local real estate market.

Mom didn't drive, so she asked Don if he would take her to the Wildcat section of town. Here Mom explained to Don that a superhighway was coming through the area and she wanted to buy some land that the Government would later need.

Don told me that she would ask him to pull over. After getting out she would survey the area. One time she got back into the car and told Don, "I think I found the place. Now, if someone were wanting to build a highway through these parts, I would think that they would pretty much have to come through this hollow right here." Now Don had grown to greatly admire my mother, but even he was pretty skeptical about her investing in a piece of land out in the middle of nowhere.

After checking the county records she found out who owned land in that area. It so happens that the acreage she wanted – ten acres in all with a small house better described as a shack on the land – belonged to one man. She bought the land, kit and caboodle, for two thousand dollars. Aside from the ramshackle house, the land also had an artesian well! This really appealed to Mom. She insured the house for a thousand dollars.

Just over a year later, a highway engineer came to see Mom. "Mrs. Martin?" he said. "Our records show that you own some land near the Jefferson National Forest. You probably know that we plan to build an interstate highway through this area. We are prepared to make you an offer for a small piece of your property."

Mom asked what the offer was. Mom said she nearly fainted when he said three thousand dollars for just over one acre of the ten she had purchased just three years before!

She quietly replied that this was a fair offer. The engineer was astounded "Mrs. Martin," he exclaimed. "People usually act insulted when we make an offer. Thank you for being so reasonable!"

The house had been occupied by squatters. Mom was charging them ten dollars a month for rent, but I don't believe she ever collected a cent! Then the bad news came.

Winky Whitt, our insurance man, called to say the house had burnt down. Nothing left but ashes. Where did he want Mom's check for a thousand dollars sent? Naturally, she was glad to have gotten rid of the dump since it had been vacant for many months. To top it off, she still had over eight acres left to sell. She thought she would hold off doing that until the highway was built since the value would probably increase even more!

Mrs. Martin Buys a Swamp

At the foot of Poplar Hill, the land was very marshy. Because of this, no houses were built on the acre or more of land there.

A lady in Richmond, Virginia inherited the track and called Mom. Actually, she called the Postmaster in Big Stone Gap who happened to be Mom. She asked Mom if she was familiar with the area. Naturally, Mom told her she had grown up in the area and knew exactly where the land was.

The lady then asked Mom if she knew of anyone who might be interested in purchasing the land. To her surprise, my mother said that *she* might be interested. She then asked the lady how much she wanted for it. Two thousand dollars was her response, adding that the land was very wet and she had been told that there was no way for it to be drained and made useable. Mom told her the price sounded very reasonable and she was aware of the water problem. So they made a deal.

Word quickly spread that Mrs. Martin really did it this time. She'd bought a swamp!

Several of the more prominent men in town chuckled at the story. One of them was John Holmes, an engineer who owed a quarry and was very knowledgeable about land.

At Uncle John's drug store, I witnessed a discussion Mom had with Mr. Holmes. "Glessie," he said. "Before I built my house [which was nearby], I took a good look at that land. I firmly believe that there are several small streams feeding the area. It would be almost impossible to divert them all so the land could dry off."

"Well, John, I know J.J. Kelly also built a beautiful home at the foot of Poplar Hill.

"But Glessie," he countered. "They built a raised road that separates his land from your property. It created a dam of a sort so he could build."

"I still think that one stream is the reason and if I can find and divert it, the rest of the land would dry out."

A few weeks later Mom hired a man with a bulldozer. He met her on the raised road next to the swamp. A bunch of us kids gathered around the dozer. Mom was paying the fellow $14 an hour! What an unbelievable sum of money since, at 14 years old, I was making 35 cents an hour!

I'll never forget the sight as long as I live. Here was Mom taking off her shoes, hoisting her skirt and wading into the marsh. She trudged about a hundred feet back and forth looking intently at the ground.

The man on the bulldozer sat with a doubting look on his face shaking his head. The motor on the dozer was idling.

Pretty soon, Mom motioned to the man. She pointed to a spot and directed him through the path he should take. The fellow put the blade down and started moving dirt in the direction that Mom gestured. It didn't take long for him to hit a single stream. The one that fed the marsh!

Once that stream was diverted, the land started drying off. I don't remember how long it took, but by the next spring the land was suitable to build on. Turned out she was able to make about 16 lots, which Mom sold for $3,000 each.

Not a bad profit for buying swampland.

Cool, Clear Water

In the 1940s, if you told someone that you were going to bottle water and sell it, people would think you were nuts! I'm not talking about Perrier or any fancy imported mineral water. I'm talking about water from limestone caves. Cool, untreated, natural water.

It was about 1949 when I came home on leave from Virginia Tech. At supper mother announced that she had just bought Kennedy cave, which was on the side of Wallen's Mountain.

"You *what*?" I exclaimed. "You bought a cave?"

I think just about everybody in Big Stone Gap had explored Kennedy cave. It had narrow passages, huge rooms with pools of clear great tasting limestone water. In those days, we mostly used carbide lamps on a miner's hat, leaving our hands free to negotiate the rough terrain of the cave.

"Why?" I asked.

"You know the limestone water in the cave is abundant. I believe there will come a day when this county will need untreated, fresh water!" she replied.

I still wanted to know more about the transaction so I began questioning further.

"How many acres on the mountainside did you buy?" I asked.

I don't remember her response, but she did say it went from the foot of the mountain to the top – maybe 200 yards wide. Quite a swath – which included the cave. She paid about $6,000 for the whole thing.

About a year later on another leave from Virginia Tech, I told mother I had talked to a business law professor at Tech. I explained to her his reaction when I told him about Kennedy cave. "He says you have, in insurance terms, "an attractive nuisance." If it was open to the public and someone fell or was injured, you could be sued.

"Oh, dear," Mom sadly replied. "I was not aware of that. So many people have been through that cave. I can't recall anyone ever suing." The next day she called Winky Whitt, her insurance man, and he confirmed what I had reported.

A couple of months later, I returned from school for another visit home. At suppertime, Mom announced that she sold Kennedy cave. I felt a great sense of relief come over me since I had been the one to sound the alarm.

"Did I tell you about the stand of walnut trees on the land?"

"No, Mom, you didn't."

"Well," she continued, "This lumber company contacted me sometime back about buying the walnut trees. I was reluctant to sell because I really believed this country one day would need plain old water!"

"They offered me $12,000, which at first I declined. After a while I told them I would take $16,000 and threw in all the land – including the cave. They accepted."

People buying bottled water? Lots of luck, dreamer!

The Later Years

Dad told me that, as a high school freshman, he once found himself looking through a bunch of his school's old yearbooks while stuck in detention after class. He started going through all the senior biographies where they listed their various extracurricular activities – varsity sports, choir, Glee Club, etc. He eventually found the student with the highest number of activities of any graduate of Big Stone Gap High. He decided at that moment that he would make it his personal ambition to beat that number before he graduated. He signed up for everything he could. By the end of his senior year, he had achieved his goal and still somehow managed to graduate. I'm not sure if his record still stands, but you can tell from the following stories that, as busy as he was, he still managed to find time for some notable adventures.

Working on the Farm

Paul McConnell's grandfather owned around 300 acres about five miles from Pound, Virginia. Aside from the family garden, they grew corn and hay as their staple crops. It was during World War II and I was about 13 years old when Paul asked me if I would like to work with him on his granddad's farm. Pay was never mentioned.

Since I had no desirable job offers for the summer, I decided it might be fun. My current after-school job was keeping Mr. McCormick's garden weeded and keeping the chicken coop and the barn clean. For this work I was being paid 35 cents an hour. Anything, I thought, had to be better. I had never lived on a primitive farm.

No running water, no electricity, no sewer system, no shower. What was I thinking! Plus the fact I was subjected to more religion than my soul could handle.

Paul's granddad was a retired Methodist Circuit rider who pastored small churches in southwest Virginia. His mode of transportation was a horse. His pay was dependent upon the generosity of the country churches and the hospitality of the congregation. Needless to say, he was a devoted Christian who lived by the Word.

At my first morning breakfast with Paul's family, I had just reached for the plate of biscuits when he started praying. I was still holding the plate when he said "Amen." He looked up at me and said it was gracious of me to offer the Lord some biscuits, but he didn't think the Lord was hungry. Everyone was laughing and I was really embarrassed.

Every night except Wednesday and Sunday, we had Vespers or a daily devotional at sunset. On Wednesday, we journeyed into Pound for vespers and evening services. On Sunday it was Sunday school, church, return home for a scrumptious meal, return to church for vespers and 7:30 service. By late Sunday night I was up to my eyeballs with Methodism.

But, I didn't go to the farm for religious training; I was there to learn the joy of hoeing corn, stacking hay, and other farm requirements. I've never worked so hard in all my life. The two horses worked hard too – plowing, pulling the hay wagon, and dragging the hay mower. I know they looked forward to the end of the day when we would take them to the riverbank to drink and have us splash water on them to cool off. At the same time we went swimming to cool off and bathe.

One of the mares was named "Ol' Jim." Oh well, she didn't know the difference! Ol' Jim had a razorback, that is, her spine was sticking up kinda like a triangular ridge down her back.

It was a hot, sweltering summer day and I was dog-tired, so I decided to ride Ol' Jim to the river. The mare had worked all day too. When I mounted her razorback I could immediately tell that was not a smart decision on my part. I was barely aboard when she takes off in a full gallop across a plowed field.

I clung to her neck with my life! Talk about rough ride! She did everything except rear up trying to throw me off. Finally, we reached the river. Ol' Jim kept moving her head up and down. Dumb me, I reined in on her. She gave me plenty of slack. All of a sudden she thrust her head forward in a violent move and off I went sailing through the air. I must have done a somersault because I landed flat on my back in the river.

Do you think horses can laugh? I, for one, know they can. When I turned around she seemed to be grinning from ear to ear! I never rode that old mare again!

As I said, life on the farm was hard but we still enjoyed some pleasures. One pleasure was riding down the mountain on a small railroad car the sawmill used to bring tree trunks to the mill. We would unhitch the cars from the coal tender and laboriously – and I mean laboriously – push the cars up the mountain. On top we would jump aboard and let gravity take its course. There was a kind of break on the car. It was a long handle sticking straight up and the break pad pushed against the wheels to slow it down. One of the bigger men would act as "breakman" since it took a lot of power to slow it down – especially when we neared the mill. I would say it was 'bout as good as a roller coaster because it was so scary to ride.

Another thing I learned: A toss in the hay is not what its cracked up to be (no pun intended). A group of kids from the church came over to the house for a picnic. One of the girls I was "sweet on" and I went to the barn and climbed to the loft.

We started fooling around and pretty soon we were semi-naked. Soon briars and stickers in the hay started pricking us. Our lovemaking was punctuated by "ouch! That hurt!" Passion started wearing off when the pain took over. A lesson learned.

On most Saturday afternoons, we would walk into the little village of Pound. Thank goodness they had a theater. We didn't care what movie was playing; we were just delighted to get away from the farm. Sometimes we didn't leave the theater until it was dark. The first part of our journey back home wasn't too bad because we could feel the asphalt road beneath our feet. But once we were on the gravel road, visibility became much more difficult. Even with a full moon we had to walk slowly to "feel" the road. That was our penalty for staying at the movies so late.

Late in July I started getting homesick. School would be starting early in September. Also I planned to go out for football and the two-a-day practice sessions began late in August. I wanted the few free days in August for myself. No more getting up at 5:30, a real bathroom, sleeping in my own room, no chores, electricity, no chopping wood, no hoeing corn or stacking hay. I wanted civilization!

Working for the Mr. McCormick didn't seem so bad and I was glad to get 35 cents an hour.

On the plus side, I learned the hardship of working on a farm. It surely was honest work with no frills. I felt great! Had a "beach" tan. There is much to be said about healthy living on a farm … but you'll never get me on one again!

Floyd B. Root

I think it was my sophomore year in high school when Mom told me that a dance instructor, Mr. Floyd B. Root from Kingsport, Tennessee, wanted to start a ballroom dance class once a week for, I believe, ten weeks. She thought it would be nice for me to learn to waltz, swing dance, and rumba. Although I was not good at it, I still liked to dance. It was a great way not only to meet girls, but also to razzle-dazzle 'em with my fancy footwork … and Mom was paying for it!

We met after school, about 4:00 p.m. at the Community League Club House, which had a large open area. About ten girls and four boys showed up. We first began with the two-step and progressed to other, more complicated dance routines.

After about the third week, Mr. Root asked two older girls – sisters – and me to meet with him after class. He said he wanted to start a class in Appalachia about three miles from Big Stone Gap and asked if we would help him. I would take one girl and he the other and would demonstrate some of the steps he had taught us. I was flattered that he asked me since I was convinced I had two left feet.

It was in late fall and, after the Tuesday class, which was over about five, we were to go to Appalachia. He had scheduled our performance for 7:00 p.m. In the time between, he said he wanted us to practice our routines.

Our show seemed to go over very well. At least I didn't trip over my partner's feet or screw up as I usually did. We left Appalachia shortly after 9:00 p.m.

About halfway between the two towns is Roaring Branch, a scenic water stream that comes winding down the mountain. There was no road, but an area just large enough to drive a car into and be off the highway. This is just what he did. He then cut the engine and turned off the headlights. It was pitch black.

The next thing I knew, I heard the girl in the front seat pleading "Please don't do that, Mr. Root. Please stop!" I couldn't see what he was doing, but I could guess. In my "manly" 14-year-old voice, I squeaked, "You better not do that, Mr. Root!"

To my surprise, he started the engine and quickly backed out onto the road and headed for Big Stone. Not a word was said as he drove at breakneck speed. Coming to an abrupt halt in the center of town, without saying anything we rushed to get out of the car. He then sped off.

The girls thought I was a hero. Little did they know I was scared as hell! We never heard from Mr. Root again. Mom was mad because she had paid for my dance lessons in advance. Many times I was asked if I knew what happened to Mr. Root and many times I just answered, "I dunno!"

The Snake Handler

The snake handlers were a different sect – an offshoot of a religious group that used a text from the Bible to justify their belief in Jesus. As I understand, the verse is from Mark 16 – "They shall take up serpents; and if they drink any deadly thing, it shall not hurt them…" This was the part they used to justify their belief that they could pick up snakes with their hands and drink deadly poison without fear of harm.

The State of Virginia, however, did not agree. They said it was an unlawful act to handle snakes or drink poisonous substances like Strychnine.

Rumor had it that the sect was going to have a "revival" – if that is a proper way to describe their determination to flaunt the law. The revival was to take place in St. Charles, Virginia – a mining town Southwest of Big Stone Gap right next to the Virginia/Kentucky border. Johnny Holmes and I wanted to see all the excitement, so we thumbed a ride. After two rides, we approached St. Charles. Out in a field was a gathering of people surrounding three old cars of early '30s vintage. Preachers (I suppose they were preachers) were yelling and jumping up and down on the car roofs testifying with loud shouts about their love of God.

When we arrived that hot Sunday afternoon, we found the crowd was beginning to get worked up. Virginia State Troopers seemingly came out of nowhere and stood in a large group away from the crowd. Besides their gun belts, guns and holsters, they carried clubs, which looked to be about three feet long and a couple of inches in diameter. I think they were called nightsticks.

It was a hot, humid day and after a while, because of all the shouting, gospel singing and clapping of hands, the preachers began to take off their coats. For over two hours we had been waiting for the snakes to appear. With all their fervor and stomping up and down to proclaim their message, I could see the car tops were really taking a beating.

About an hour later, one of the preachers yelled out, "Now let the snakes appear!" Johnny and I found ourselves being pushed toward the cars. Standing in front of me was a very large, tall woman.

All of a sudden, the snakes came out! The preachers had them in their shirts! They would take a snake, usually a copperhead, hold it with one hand high above their head and start praying very loudly. Then they brought the snakes to eye level and began to try to kiss them on their heads. They handed the snakes down to the eagerly awaiting hands of people who would do the same thing then hand it to the next person.

My eyes were fixed on a young woman, probably in her early twenties, over to my left. She was weaving back and forth like she was in a trance. So you can imagine my shock when this big fat lady standing in front of me threw what I thought was a snake over her shoulder and the end hit my face. I could feel the fangs bite into my check!

Frantically, I started rubbing my face with both hands in hopes the venom wouldn't spread and bolted to get outside the crowd. "I've been bit!" I cried out. Johnny chased me and nabbed my arms, laughing at me hysterically.

"Damn it, Johnny, I've been bit!" My own friend didn't care that I had been mortally wounded!

Johnny had witnessed the whole thing. The fat lady had been making a long braid with her hair. After she finished, she stuck it with a bobby pin to hold it together and tossed it over her shoulder. That's when it hit my face. After he wrestled me to the ground, he was laughing so hard that he had a rough time telling me it wasn't a snake. Finally, I started to calm down and I got up. I no longer felt the pain and swelling. Grabbing me by the arm, he pulled me toward the fat lady. Sure enough – there was the braid and at the end was a bobby pin – I mean the two fangs – sticking out!

But my troubles were far from over. Away from the crowd, while trying to slow my beating heart, I had noticed a man standing beside me. He took my arm with both hands. He had on a white shirt, no tie, no hat and had a frightening look in his eyes.

"What now?" I thought, "Why me, Lord?"

"Don't let them take my snake!" he yelled into my ears.

I tried to unleash myself from his grasp while looking all around for the snake. In this panicked state I noticed that the state troopers had encircled us. "Get outta there boy!" they yelled.

Try as I could, the maniac had me in a vice grip! One trooper crept up behind the man, quickly grabbed his collar and the back of his shirt, and violently pulled him down. His shirt opened and a copperhead came falling out, striking the ground at our feet.

I can't remember what my attacker did, but I danced! ("Hopped around wildly" might be a better description.)

The troopers closed in. Finally, I was able to break away temporarily with the assistance of the cops. Their long nightsticks were flailing away at the poor snake. The snake went flying in the air and the troopers tried to hit like they were in a baseball game. When one of them got a good hit, the snake happened to sail towards other troopers and there was much animation. It reminded me of a scene from an old Keystone Kops movie. After a while it was quite evident the snake was dead.

I had had enough excitement for the day. Johnny, however, was not ready to leave.

I walked over to the base of a hill. Sitting on the ground under a tree was a man with his head down. His two arms were extended supported by his knees. He was moaning, "God will save me, God will save me!" Then he looked up and saw me. "Joe Gordon" he said painfully. "I've been bit!"

It was Mr. Lambert, the father of a schoolmate of mine. He then held out one hand toward me. It was swollen – especially at the base of the thumb. Carefully looking I could see the fang marks. "Mr. Lambert," I asked, "Can I get you a doctor?"

"No! No!" he replied. "The Lord will save me!"

With that, I went to search for Johnny. I had enough and wanted to go home.

Later I learned that a pharmacist, "Junebug White," had lanced the wound and Mr. Lambert lived.

Turns out I was cured too – of any desire to go to another revival!

The Basketball Manager versus Luther Updyke

Two brothers, "Uppy" Updyke and his younger brother, Luther, both played sports. Uppy was a very good basketball player. Luther, was a good player, but not as good as his brother. To me, Luther was a royal pain in the ass! Unlike Uppy, he had an aloofness about him that struck me as being better than you. You guessed it – I didn't like him.

After one game our team went into the locker room to quickly shower and dress. Luther came to me and, in a demanding voice said, "I have a jock itch. What have you got for it!" Jock itch was a common ailment that occurred when sweaty parts of your lower body rubbed together causing a rash.

We had just gotten a bottle of Tuff-Skin, which was a new product that you put on calluses to shield them from becoming blistered. But you dared not put the ointment on an open blister or sore; it burned like hell.

"Yes, sir, Luther," I eagerly responded. "I've got just the thing for you. Just apply this over the itchy area."

I went about my job, picking up discarded towels and such, when a scream let out from Luther's direction. There he was, hopping around like a madman. I don't know what he was thinking, but he ran out of the locker room directly into the basketball court – naked as a jaybird! Jumping up and down, cursing, his eyes tightly closed – he was a sight to behold. The pain tapered off and he opened his eyes. Not everyone had left the gym. Luther raced into the locker room saying some really unkind things about me.

Professor J. Roy Horne

Our school principal's name was J. Roy Horne. "Professor Horne" was what we called him. He was a big, powerful man who didn't take guff from anybody, and that included teachers, parents, city officials – and especially students. We lived in God-fear of being called into his office. I really respected the man and tried to avoid anything that would put me in close proximity to him.

Every Wednesday he left school to attend the Kiwanis Club luncheon meeting. Usually he left about 11:30 a.m. and did not return until after 1:00 p.m. He had just hired a new college graduate, Miss Slemp, as a secretary who doubled as the typing teacher. She sat across from him in his big office.

Professor Horne had left for Kiwanis and I was gathering some kids together for a meeting about the school's yearbook, for which I was the editor. I happened to pass the principal's office and, glancing in, saw Miss Slemp. Feeling my oats, I marched in and told Miss Slemp that I needed the office and that she would have to do her work elsewhere.

Obediently, she got up, lugging a huge typewriter down the steps. I heard those words that Professor Horne would say when he was surprised at something. "Hello, Pete! What are you doing, Miss Slemp?"

"Joe Martin said they were going to use your office for a meeting and I should work someplace else!"

"We'll see about that." And here he came.

My committee members disappeared. I sat at Miss Slemp's seat and pretended to review some documents. There he stood along with Ms. Stemp who had a strained look from carrying the typewriter. "Hi, Professor. I'm waiting on my committee to discuss our yearbook." I said breezily.

"Set that typewriter down, Miss Slemp. And you, Joe Gordon, get your things together and get out of my office! I'll see you later!" he added.

Later never came. Every time he saw me, something came up and he was diverted from killing me.

Around this time, we got a new football coach, Joe Starnes, who had played football at West Point. I don't remember if he ever served in the Army after graduating. I think he stayed on at the Point as an assistant coach. Anyway, he landed at Big Stone Gap High School – the "Home of the Buccaneers."

This man was a taskmaster. He was muscular and personally led the team calisthenics. At the beginning of the football season in August, he had two-a-day practice sessions.

I thought I was going to die. Between practices, all I could do was go home, drink a little something and lie on the couch until it was time to go at it again. Seems like every afternoon I would barf anything that was on my stomach. Sweat poured off me. The sun was unmerciful. Coach Starnes was determined to whip us into shape or "we" would die trying.

Coach Starnes also had new ideas about the type of formation we would be learning. Heretofore, we had the employed single wing. His Army football team used a split-tee formation. Quite a difference!

Some of us began to rebel: "Why are we taking this? We don't have to play football! To hell with Starnes, his split-tee, his workouts – the whole damn thing! We'll quit. That'll show him!" So we did.

Out of a squad of 33 players, eight walked out. Half were on first string and four of us were second-string players. The next day we didn't show up for practice.

That night Mom sent me to Uncle John's drug store to pick something up. When I went in, I didn't notice at first who was talking to Uncle John. That is, until I heard that familiar phrase – "Hello Pete!"

I cringed. Of all the people I didn't want to see, he was number one.

"Joe Gordon," he called out. "I understand that some of you boys don't want to play football."

"Yes, sir," I managed to get the words out of my throat.

"Let me tell you something," he said. Then he began a recitation.

"Coach Starnes talked me into getting new uniforms for you boys. You got new shoes, didn't you?" I nodded my head. "They cost..." and he proceeded to name the cost down to the penny, though I don't recall it now. "You have new jerseys with big bright gold letters. The jerseys cost... We got rid of those canvas pants. Now you have gold nylon pants with the blue stripe down the side... How about those new plastic helmets? The old leather ones are gone. They we're kind of pricey at over $13 each. Now you add up the figures and it comes to over $25 I spent on each one of you so you could play football.

"You know, Joe Gordon, I don't waste the school's money. I would suggest you call your fellow quitters and tell them what I told you."

"Yes, sir," I managed to say and I made a hasty retreat out the door and completely forgot what Mom had sent me there for in the first place.

At home I made the calls. The next day eight changed boys showed up for practice. And the Coach still showed no mercy.

Coach Fitchko

This is one of a couple of stories I have about William T. Fitchko. He was from Pittsburgh, Pennsylvania and played football at the University of Pittsburgh. After that he played professional football under the famous coach, Jock Sutherland. He was their kicker and punt man – evidently a good one at that. But, this story is not about football; it's about one of the dumbest things I have ever done. As you read this story, I'm sure you will agree.

My junior year in high school, I was the basketball manager. Basically, my duties were to take care of our equipment and haul it in and out of our storage room, take care of the boy's locker room (though I didn't have to clean it – the janitor did that), and be ready with the first aid kit.

One Friday night we played at Norton, Virginia. The night before, their gym had been broken into and among the things stolen were their basketballs. Since we were playing on their home court, I took six basketballs. Normally we would use about three or four during the warm-ups. Their manager told me of their plight. They could muster up only one ball, so I lent him two of ours.

The next day in the equipment storage room Coach Fitchko and I were taking inventory. "Hey, Joe," he called out. "We're missing two balls."

"Oh yeah, Coach," I explained. "I loaned them to Norton's manager. Their locker room had been broken into and their basketballs were stolen."

"Who in the hell told you you could do that?" he demanded.

"Well, Coach, we didn't need them for practice so I figured we could help them out." I could not for the life of me understand why he got so mad. He didn't ease up and continued to chew me out. Now I was getting mad. "I'll go to Norton and get those damn balls," I shouted out.

"Don't you talk back to me," he countered.

"I'm not talking back, I'm telling you I'll be responsible for those damn balls," I said again in a shouting voice.

I can't recall the words that were exchanged that provoked him to say, "Looks like you'd like to put on the gloves with me."

"Damn right I would!" I defiantly said. What a big mistake.

On the wall hung two pairs of boxing gloves. One pair he threw at me, the other he put on. Neither of us tied the laces.

All I can remember is that I tried to lay a haymaker on him and he hit me in the face, which slammed me against the wall. I don't know whether it was his punch or me hitting the wall that knocked me out. The only thing I remember is seeing him down on the floor gently slapping me on both cheeks trying to arouse me. Later that afternoon, the coach and I went to Norton and picked up those damn balls.

I was in pain for the rest of the weekend and could tell that I had a loose tooth. So on Monday, I went to see Dr. Strader, the dentist, who informed me that the tooth was not going to make it and would have to come out. Then he got to work on me.

Now it so happened that, during school on the day before the basketball game, Sue Reasor, a cute, feisty girl, slapped me in the same place where the coach later hit me. I had said something smart-alecky to her – which was no surprise – and she responded with a slap – also no surprise as it had happened before.

So when I spied Sue on Tuesday morning, I came up to her with a sour look on my face and proceeded to show her the gaping hole in my mouth. "Now look what you did!"

"I did?" she said. "Oh, I'm so sorry. Please don't tell anyone that it was my fault!" she begged. She sure was nice to me after that.

I kept the fight, if you can call it that, between the coach and me very quiet. Believe me, he was thankful for that!

After leaving Big Stone Gap High, Fitchko became the head coach in football and basketball at Norton High School. There he created a championship football team and won the district title. At the buzzer, the players, in their jubilation, hoisted Coach up on their shoulders. He grinned from ear to ear, waived a victory sign to the crowd and then died right on the spot. What a way for a coach to leave this earth.

Christmas Caroling in Big Stone Gap

It must have been my senior year in high school when a group of young people from our church decided to go Christmas caroling. Since it was a cold night, I figured some of us guys would need a little warmth to help our vocal cords. So I filled up a small fruit jar with whiskey.

One of the unscheduled stops we made was at Reverend Russell Asbury's house. The right Rev. Asbury didn't care much for me, but I was with a group. So when he invited us in for a cup of hot chocolate, I dutifully followed the group into his parsonage.

He instructed us to stash our winter coats in the master bedroom, which was on the first floor. When I began taking off my coat, I smelled something. Whiskey had seeped through the lid of the fruit jar! Well, I did what every red-blooded sinner would do under similar circumstances – I sprinkled whiskey on everyone else's coats.

After the hot chocolate, we began filing out when one girl remarked, "What's that funny smell?" I quickly ushered her out the front door.

Nothing was ever said about that night, at least to my knowledge. But it probably reinforced Rev. Asbury's opinion of me.

Borrowing Rev. Asbury's Car

The Rev. Asbury had two very pretty daughters. One was my age and the other about three years older. I saw the older one, Bette, in Carmine's (the local hangout) and asked her if she would like to go to the Kopper Kettle, or let me put it this way: "Hey, Bette, why don't you get your daddy's car and let's you and me go to the Kettle!"

She responded, "I'd love to go, Joe Gordon, but you have got to call Daddy and ask to use his car to take me."

"Sure I will!" I confidently replied. "Matter of fact, I'll call him tonight!"

"What time?" she asked.

"Seven o'clock. Be sure to call me earlier if he won't be home at that time."

Bette called me at home to confirm that her father would be home that evening. Truth is, I wasn't about to call Rev. Asbury. There was no doubt in my mind that he would love to chew me out for even thinking of such an idea.

However, right about seven the phone rang in the Parsonage. Rev. Asbury answered it, having been alerted by Bette to expect a call from yours truly. The conversation went something like this: "Good evening, Pastor," the voice started out saying. "I'm sorry I missed going to church last Sunday."

"You're sorry, alright! You're about the sorriest thing in this town," he replied emphatically.

"Well Pastor," the voice lamented. "I try to go every Sunday, but I just couldn't get there because –"

The Rev. Asbury cut him off. "It would take many Sundays for you to repent!"

"Pastor, could I talk to you after prayer meeting Wednesday night?" the voice pleadingly said.

"Yes you can and you better be on your knees!"

Then the voice said something that caused Rev. Asbury to pause and ask, "Is this Joe Gordon?"

"No, sir, this is Roland Rose (one of the church deacons)."

Bette told me her father went into a state of shock. He mumbled something on the phone and quickly hung up the phone. Bette thought it sounded something like, "I'll kill him!" and stalked out of the room.

There was no further discussion about borrowing the reverend's car.

The Cabin Raid

Bill Wolfe's house sat on a long lot, the back of which ended at the side of a riverbank. Bill, Bob and Dutchy Morris, Gary and Gene Collier and I decided it was the perfect spot to build a cabin. And with Bill's father's help, we proceeded to do so.

Mr. Wolfe found some rough-cut planks from a sawmill. As I recall, we dug six postholes for our two-by-four posts. The cabin was about 12 feet long, ten feet wide and eight feet tall. It had one door, one window and a dirt floor. We built the roof using plywood sheets; it was flat and covered with tarpaper. We covered the interior walls with cardboard for insulation.

We had four bunk beds, two on each side at the rear, all framed with two-by-fours. To these we attached chop sacks or feed sacks to the inside framework that sort of sagged down to make a bed. A bit uncomfortable, but we were proud of our accomplishment. We later added a cheap, freestanding wood-burning stove for heat in the winter. The heat it provided was awesome so we didn't have to build too much of a fire. Oh yes, if we had a fifth overnight guest, we had an army issue foldout cot. A small table with a couple of folding chairs finished out our "mansion" in the woods and sufficed for our needs.

On the weekends most of us would take off for the cabin. "Let the good times roll," as they say in New Orleans!

A year or so later Mr. Wolfe decided to build a bigger and better cabin, thinking perhaps he would add a bathroom and rent it out. For the time being, it had no bathroom. It did, though, have a concrete floor, a pitched roof with shingles, and nice aluminum siding. But for the life of me I can't remember how it was heated.

We had a bed that could only sleep two and the rest slept on the floor in sleeping bags. The new cabin had a larger table and folding chairs. What a great place!

On a typical weekend, we would see if one of the town drunks would buy us some cheap wine – 65-cent Virginia Dare Muscatel would do just fine – or beer – any kind would do – a couple of six packs if we had the money. We'd pack some cheese, crackers, bologna, Duke's mayonnaise, and some light (what you'd call white) bread. Add four or five Nehis or a big RC Cola and we were ready to party! As always, the extent of the party was largely determined by the limited amount of money we had accumulated.

Every once in a while, we'd get a girl to come up there. Say a waitress at an all night café would get off work about 3:00 a.m. I would pick her up after prearranging the rendezvous and bring her to the cabin. How shall I say it? She was a real sportin' gal! Yes! Yes!

A high school classmate, Carl Jessee, asked Bill Wolfe if he could spend Friday night at the cabin. He had heard that we really had some good times up there. Bill polled the members of our group for a vote. I told them I had a date that night and would not be joining them, so there was a "vacancy." Bill reluctantly said Jessee could come. Since I was not there that night, the remainder of this story comes second hand from the rest of our gang.

Carl was, at the time, going steady with Jo Ann Nave. And when he informed her that he was spending the night at the cabin, she went ballistic! She had heard about all the bad boys and what they were doing up there in that cabin. She also told her mother who, in turn, informed Tom Fugate, the State Highway Patrolman, who happened to rent a room in the Nave's house. Tom Fugate thought it serious enough to tell Barron Lane, the Chief of Police. Thursday, Jo Ann informed Carl Jessee that he had better not go to the cabin that night because there might be big trouble. He bailed out, but never bothered to tip any of us off.

I went on my date while the others made their usual pilgrimage up to the cabin that Friday night. Just after three in the morning, Barron Lane, Tom Fugate, and Luther Edwards, the night patrol officer staged a raid on the cabin. The door burst open, the police chief in the lead.

With weapons at the ready, they piled into the room. Gary and his brother Gene had been playing penny-ante poker earlier that night and a few pennies were still on the table; these were gathered up as evidence. The place was searched for booze. According to Gary, all they found was one empty beer bottle.

The crowning achievement of the raid came when Chief Lane saw a head plopped on a pillow. You couldn't see the face, but the hair was dark and long.

He went directly to the bed and grabbed the hair, thinking it was a girl. Up came the face of Dutchy Morris. Realizing his mistake, he quickly dropped the head back onto the pillow.

Chief Lane wrote out a citation and he and his posse quickly left the building. News of "The Raid" quickly spread throughout the town. Mr. Wolfe was particularly angry that he had been awakened by the police that night to witness the results of the raid.

The boys had to appear in Municipal Court. The presiding judge was Dutchy's and Bob's uncle. When Chief Lane presented his case and the not-so-damning evidence, Judge Taylor threw out the charges and proceeded to chew out the Chief.

Carl Jessee wasn't invited to any more of our parties!

Where are You Going? Out!

I have got to tell this story. I will, however, change names to protect the guilty!

One weekend I was given leave from VPI (Virginia Polytechnic Institute – more about VPI later) to go home. I arrived in Big Stone late in the afternoon. I was about to cross the street at the Kelly Drug Corner when I hear a voice call out, "Hi, Joe!"

It was a girl I knew. Let's call her Susie Q. I was really glad to see her. She had been away at an all-girls school and was a real fun-loving gal.

I yelled back, "Whatcha doin tonight?"

She answered, "Nuthin'!"

"Let's go to the Kettle tonight!" The Kopper Kettle was a nice dance hall. You brought your own bottle of booze and bought setup (the mixers) there. Also, there was a slight cover charge.

"Great!" she replied.

"Pick you up at seven?"

"Ok!" she answered. The light changed and off she went.

At home I quickly showered, changed clothes from my VPI Cadet Uniform to civvies, and grabbed a bite to eat. I was just about to go out the front door when Mom asked, "Where are you going?"

My usual answer was, "Out." Mom would then ask, "Who are you going out with?" To which I would normally reply, "Oh, you don't know her." End of conversation.

This time was different. Now I was in college and Mom was paying the majority of the cost. She deserved a better answer. Besides that, I had no idea that Mom would really know anything about my friend Susie. In addition, she was the granddaughter of a prominent businessman in Big Stone who was good a friend of Mom's.

So, I answered her question. "I'm picking up Susie Q and we're going to the Kettle." As I answered her question, I was turning to walk out the door. I heard her slam shut the book she was reading.

"Must you embarrass me when you come home?" she asked in a demanding voice. "If you don't care about your own reputation, please, kindly consider mine!"

I froze in my tracks. I thought no one really knew about Susie's reputation.

"Gee, Mom, I briefly saw her tonight at Kelly Drug Corner and asked her to go to the Kettle! Are we talking about the same person – Mr. Q's granddaughter?" I plaintively asked.

"Yes!" she said. "We're talking about Miss Susie Q! You know what she did?"

"No, Mom, I don't! I just got into town and haven't talked to anyone except Susie."

"Surely you know!" she said, doubting my explanation.

"No, Mom, I don't know! What has she done?"

Mom proceeded to tell me the story that the whole town was talking about. "She was picked up walking down Lee County Highway by Tom Fugate, you know our state trooper assigned to Big Stone." I could only nod my head because I knew Tom Fugate.

"What had she done?" I feebly asked.

"She was drunk – and naked!" Mom sternly said. "Must you be seen with her? Can't you think of my reputation if you don't care about yours?"

"Mom, I already made a date with her and I'm late now! I promise I won't see her anymore after tonight!"

I turned and quickly left. When I arrived at her grandfather's stately home, he answered the door. "Good evening, Joe," he quickly said. He usually greeted me with a smile and a hardy hello. Tonight was different.

Susie came flying down the stairs and out the door.

"Boy, I'm sure glad to see you! I almost thought you wouldn't come!" she added.

"Yeah, I did think about it," I replied. "I understand you really ripped it!"

In the car she asked, "Do you know Poss Henry?"

"Yeah, I've heard about him."

"Well, he got me drunk on moonshine and tried to put the make on me! I told him I didn't want any part of him and got out of his car and started walking home. I was so drunk that I didn't realize I was naked!" she continued. "Then, of all the people in the world, who should stop but that damn Tom Fugate, the State Trooper.

"He gave me his uniform jacket and dropped me off at Granddaddy's. You can imagine how my life has been since then! Boy, I'm glad to see you!" she said again. "I'm ready to have a good time!"

We did! But I thought it would be prudent if I got home before midnight. I did.

Mom's light was on in her room. I quietly knocked and looked in. She was having difficulty in finding words to say to me.

I apologized profusely, promising that I would behave myself as best I could from now on when I come home for a visit.

Part 2
The College Years

Virginia Polytechnic Institute

Dad attended Virginia Polytechnic Institute (VPI – now known as Virginia Tech) as a member of the Corps of Cadets for his first two years of college beginning in 1949 before transferring to the University of Cincinnati. VPI was one of the few remaining schools today with both a civilian student body and a military component. He tells many hilarious stories of his brief time there – usually ones that end with him wiggling out of one form of trouble or another. Here are two of those stories. The first, "A Cure for Corporal Quigg," goes down in my book as the best practical joke I have ever heard.

A Cure for Corporal Quigg

From my experience, practical jokes are all about paying attention to what's happing in a given moment and finding a way to capitalize on that moment. This is the story of one of my most notorious practical jokes.

When men are in bull sessions with no women around (which is something that men will often do when women aren't around), the conversation will seek a lower level. Instead of putting women on a pedestal, they are conversationally laid prone on the ground.

My freshman roommates at Virginia Tech were Pete Delaney and Robert E. Beeler. We were in just such a bull session and it didn't take long until the conversation focused on women. Beeler matter-of-factly stated that he knew a woman, a nurse from the Middlesboro, Kentucky area, who was beautiful, had a fantastic figure and, on top of all that, was a nymphomaniac! Pete and I moved closer to Beeler to hear more about this unbelievable creature. He emphasized that she was crazy about him but he loved playing the field. When we expressed doubts about what he was telling us to believe, Beeler announced "I'll ask her to come up here!"

"Yeah, Beeler, you do that," Pete and I echoed.

"I'll do it," he said flatly.

Now at that time I was on Strict Military Probation, "SMP", which meant I was basically confined to the barracks with a couple of exceptions: I could go to class and the chow hall, attend all formations, go get my mail two times a day, go to the bathroom, walk off my demerits during the weekdays, and visit my Rat Daddy's room.

Let me explain a Rat Daddy. Mine was Bill Olinger, a senior with rank. I shined his shoes, took his laundry to the campus cleaners and performed any other menial tasks he wanted me to do.

Around this time, the cadets put on a big dance. Even though I was on SMP, I got permission to attend the dance from 8:00 p.m. to 11:00 p.m., at which time I was to return directly to the barracks. I had a date with a great girl from Radford School for Women. Naturally, I was excited about going on a date and enjoying a few hours of freedom.

About halfway through the evening, several of my classmates found me, drew me aside, and told me that Pete and Beeler were desperately looking for me and that I should go back to our room immediately. I thanked them, but after thinking about it, I decided I wasn't going to give up being with this terrific girl for some wood-smoke smelling country girl they may have cornered.

Precisely at 11:00 p.m., I entered our room. Almost in unison both Pete and Beeler yelled "Where have you been? Didn't anyone tell you we were looking for you?"

"Yeah," I said, "but I wasn't going to leave my date."

"She came here!" Pete exclaimed.

"Who came here?" I countered.

"Beeler's girlfriend!"

This story is almost unbelievable. Thirteen guys from our barracks participated in the orgy.

All the action happened in a paved parking lot that was situated on top of a steep hill behind our barracks. Beeler's girlfriend had driven to VPI from Kentucky, arriving at dusk. Beeler took her to dinner. After dinner it was dark and the fun began. Pete and Beeler asked a bunch of guys if they had seen me. They hadn't. A curious lot (and horny), they kept asking Pete and Beeler why they were looking for me. Since I had not shown up, they started cutting in some of the guys – particularly upperclassmen, not necessarily friends. The word spread like wildfire. As I said, thirteen guys partook. About 10:30 p.m., her car leaves the parking lot and it's all quiet – except for the barracks where a lot of laughter was going on.

It's now Sunday morning. I had been to breakfast formation. Pete and Beeler had gone somewhere, so I decided to visit my Rat Daddy. Olinger was in his room studying. I began to shine his shoes and, after brushing them, I went over to the sink. I did a variation of the "spit" shine. Instead of spit I used tap water to wet the application cloth.

I noticed on the side of his sink a small vial with no label that contained a reddish purple liquid. "What's this?" I asked.

Bill replied, "That's gentian violet. We use it to stain bacteria in one of my biology classes." Olinger was going into medical school from college. "Damn stuff gets on your fingers and it takes forever to wear off," he continued. "Soap won't do it." Another bit of useless trivia that I stored in my mind.

After lunch formation, I went back to my room. I couldn't go anywhere. I'd been to the bathroom and to my Rat Daddy's room. I didn't want to study, so I just paced back and forth like a caged animal.

All of a sudden, the door burst open and in walked Corporal Quigg (pronounced "kweeg"), a sophomore who seemed to take particular pleasure in abusing underclassmen. Needless to say, he wasn't what you'd call a buddy of mine. I quickly racked on a brace.

"At ease, Mr. Martin! I didn't see you on the hill last night," he said, almost as a question.

"No, sir, not me!"

"Not you…" He chuckled. "I thought she was your girlfriend."

At that moment it dawned on me – odds were Quigg had lost his virginity that night! I turned and walked to the window from which I could see the infamous hill.

"Tell me, Mr. Martin, did you know her?" I nodded my head in affirmation. "Boy, she was beautiful – and what a figure!" he excitedly exclaimed. I just nodded my head. I could hear him pacing the floor behind me. "You don't think she *has* anything, do you?"

My opening!

"Quigg, sir, it's, uh, not for me to say."

"What do you mean, Mr. Martin?"

"Can you keep a secret, Quigg, sir?"

"Sure I can," he responded. "Tell me, tell me your secret."

"Well, Quigg, sir, please keep this quiet," I pleaded. "Don't tell a soul! Quigg, sir, have you ever heard of 'Blue Balls'?"

"Blue Balls, Blue Balls," he repeated. "I think I have."

I turned around at this time and solemnly looked him in the eye and said, "Blue Balls is the slang for the ailment – I don't know the correct medical term. What happens is your balls, or I should say, your testicles, begin to swell." All this time I'm slowly opening up my cupped hands. His eyes were going wider and wider as my hands molded large round testicles. "The pain is excruciating."

Now for the hook to go with the bait. "There *is* a simple cure for it…"

"Yes, yes," agreed Quigg.

I tried to reassure him. "Her infection might have cleared up by now…"

"What is the cure?" he demanded.

"If I was to tell you and you went to a pharmacy in town, they'd want to know what you we're going to use this for. If you told them, rest assured they would get word to the Commandant and you and a dozen other guys would be dismissed from VPI. You can't go to the infirmary. Once again, they'd have to report it."

At this point Quigg is frantic.

"Quigg, sir, have you ever heard of gentian violet?" I asked.

"Gentian violet? Gentian violet?" he kept repeating. Finally, he admitted he had heard of it but had no knowledge about it.

I snapped my fingers – an "idea"! "We're in luck! Sergeant Olinger has some. You know he's preparing to go to med school and they use it in the laboratory to kill bacteria, which is what Blue Balls is caused by. I remember seeing some sitting on his sink last time I was shining his shoes. It's probably still there. To use it, you'll need to put it all over your privates. But you dare not tell him what you're gonna use it for!"

"No, no, I won't!" he said as he raced to get out of my room.

Once again, I was pacing the floor and Pete and Beeler had not returned. About 4:00 p.m., the door burst open and a familiar voice cried out, "At ease, Rat!" It was Olinger! "That knucklehead Quigg came bursting into my room without knocking, ran over to the sink and grabbed that bottle of gentian violet and raced out of the room. Said he was going to stain some bacteria or something!" I then told Olinger the whole story. He gave me a look and left my room.

It wasn't five minutes later when he came back in. He was laughing so hard that he had to sit down. He found Quigg lying on the top bunk naked as a jaybird with purple all around his groin.

Word spread quickly. It didn't take Quigg too long to find me and threaten to "bone me out of the corps!" As I said, I was already on SMP and any additional demerits would be cause for my dismissal. Here's where Rat Daddies come in handy. Olinger told Quigg that for every demerit Quigg gave me, he would give Quigg three.

Quigg knew he was beat. My victory was all the sweeter knowing that he (and everyone else) would be reminded of it every morning in the showers for weeks to come.

Placement Tests for the Undecided

In my second year at Virginia Polytechnic Institute, I began to have serious doubts about being in college. Strangely enough, I achieved the rank of corporal out of a company M class of 40 – only 13 of us achieved the stripes. I guess the upper classmen figured I had broken so many of the military and Rat (first year cadet) rules that I could just look at a freshman cadet and tell what was on his mind! Even so, I still didn't like the military life. I didn't even like school.

I was enrolled in the business school and found myself continually daydreaming through the classes. Accounting was something that I especially hated – even though it was so important for a business major.

There was a new guidance counselor on the campus, so I decided to talk to him. He acted as though he was delighted to see me. No wonder - he had just received a whole battery of new tests, with IQ and aptitude questions, like, "Which would you rather do – play baseball or fly a kite?" I was his guinea pig.

For several days I took IQ tests or other tests to uncover my druthers. After a week or so had gone by, he left word in my barracks for me to come in and see him. When I walked into his office I felt depressed. I really didn't think I belonged in college, but then again, I didn't know what I really wanted to do. I wasn't getting anywhere in life.

When I sat down before him, he looked me in the eye and asked, "What did you say your problem was?"

The question took me aback. "I told you – I didn't think I was smart enough to be in college!"

"You're smart enough all right!" he replied. "IQ tests proved that. Your aptitude tests showed that you really didn't care for the business courses you were taking. It also pointed out that you probably don't work well with authority or with rules and regulations. You appear to be an individualist in your views and actions." I couldn't help but agree with those observations and I told him so.

"Let me tell you a story that might help you. It's about me, but it illustrates that you can make a change in your life and be happier." He then began to share this wonderful story. It has always meant a lot to me, so now I'll share it with you.

"You know me as a guidance counselor. In that capacity you probably think I majored in psychology or even psychiatry. I didn't. My degree is in chemical engineering! After graduating from college, I had this great opportunity to work for an American oil company in Venezuela. It sounded so exciting to me.

"After the first year I wasn't so excited. I found I really didn't like what I was doing. After my second year there, WWII started and I volunteered for the Navy. I was assigned to a small destroyer escort. Our job was to accompany convoys to

Europe and keep a lookout for German subs. I was an executive officer and was next in command to the Captain, who was not much older than me.

"Out in the Atlantic a sudden storm blew up. Waves were so high they would engulf our little ship. Even ships in the convoy were having trouble. Some of the freighters were carrying so much cargo that the additional water was causing them to sink as their crews struggled to pump the water out fast enough. Our ship was receiving SOS calls for help. To top it all off, the Captain was in his quarters – seasick!

"I was now on the bridge in command! The helmsman was yelling at me for instructions and all I could do was to hold on to the railing and watch as each wave came over us! Is this the one to capsize us? I was literally scared to death."

He paused here and asked, "Mr. Martin, have you ever been so scared that your knees knocked together? So scared that you were speechless? I was all those things and more!"

Again he paused in his story. "Do you believe in God?" he asked. "You don't have to answer that, but I do." And he went on with his story.

"All of a sudden everything got still and quiet. A voice said to me, 'What are you afraid of?'

"Back to reality as another big wave engulfed us. We're going down and now I'm going crazy! I'm hearing voices!

"A second time the voice said, 'What are you afraid of?'

"This must be what it's like when you're going crazy, I thought for a second or two – then back to the storm, which was still raging. The third time the voice said, 'What are you afraid of?' Then the voice added 'You don't know when you are going to die. So what are you afraid of?'

"Suddenly, I felt this calmness – an inner peace. I didn't know when the next wave would sink us, but I wasn't going to be scared anymore. I pushed myself back from the railing that I was gripping so hard. I took over the helm, relieving the young sailor who looked as scared as I had been.

"After a couple of hours, the storm began subsiding. Meanwhile, I managed to steer the ship over to the men who were floundering in the high seas. We were able to rescue many seamen.

"When we returned to our homeport, I was personally congratulated by our Base Commander. Later came a citation and a medal for "bravery." I couldn't believe it! As far as I'm concerned, God deserved that medal. He gave me the strength to do my job.

"The reason I'm telling you this is because it changed my life. After leaving the Navy, I decided to go back to college. I learned about helping people, guiding them, and reassuring them. I found my calling.

"From what I've learned about you, you have yet to find your niche. My advice is to think about sales or something in public relations. Those areas appear to be your strong points."

It only took 15 years for me to practice that! That's when I finally went into real estate. And the rest, as they say, is history!

University of Cincinnati

After transferring from VPI, Dad attended the University of Cincinnati, graduating in 1956 with a BS in Advertising Design. It was during this time that he met my mother, Sonia. They were married on September 1st, 1956. They both knew what it meant to be poor – she having grown up in Cincinnati where her mother raised her and her two siblings mostly on her own. Dad used every tool in his bag of tricks to win Mom over.

To illustrate this point one year for a Sunday School class, Mom put together a poster showing all of the handmade cards Dad had created for her during their courtship on the left half of the poster and all the cards he made after they were married on the right. On the left were some of the most creative and funny cards you can imagine – all hand drawn and lettered, including caricatures of them both. On the right – nothing!

Despite the lack of personalized cards, Mom must have found something worthwhile in Dad that made her stick around. They celebrated 50 years of marriage in 2006 with many friends and family joining in the festivities.

Gettin' Cultchur

Going from Big Stone Gap to Cincinnati was a cultural shock. What a city! Across the river was Newport, Kentucky – wide open! Gambling, prostitution, vices of every kind. And on the other side was the Queen City – sophisticated, conservative, full of dowagers, and rich in quality theater and opera.

So, I decided I should get some exposure to the finer things and go to an opera. It was at the Cincinnati Zoo, believe it or not. The pavilion was near the birdhouses and when a trumpeter played a short tune to herald the opening, many of the birds chimed in!

The opera was *Carmen*. I figured that would introduce me to the real thing since I had heard only excerpts of it such as the Toreador song.

My seat was at the rear – the cheap seats, so to speak. On stage I thought I saw one my fraternity brothers, Ken Wood. I strained my eyeballs, but couldn't determine if it was really him. So, during intermission, I went around to the rear. The back lot was surrounded by a privacy fence, but standing on my tiptoes I could see just over the fence. Sure enough, it was Ken Wood. I hollered and he came over. "What are you doing?" I asked. "Are you a singer?"

"Nope," he replied. "I'm a supernumerary."

"A what?" I asked.

"An extra," he explained. "I'm part of a crowd scene or a soldier, whatever they need."

"You get *paid* for this?" I asked.

"Nah, I get two free tickets for another performance of another opera. You interested?" he asked.

"Sure!" I replied.

"I'll introduce you to the stage manager," he said, motioning for me to come to the gate. The manager did not have time to talk to me then, but asked that I come back after the opera ended.

I filled out an application and was asked if I could be there the next night for another performance of *Carmen*.

What fun! I was a soldier! Appearing as the star was Roberta Peters – a beautiful opera singer. I stood with my sword next to her at the cigarette factory scene.

During the opera season, I appeared in other plays. At the performance of *Aida*, I was a throne guard. Helen Traubel was the guest star. I stood at attention with my spear, wearing an Egyptian headdress, loincloth and sandals. Ms. Traubel sang a beautiful aria pleading for the life of her lover. At the end, she flung herself on the throne.

She was a rather large woman and in the process of her dramatic plea, she fell into me and knocked me thru the backdrop. Thank goodness it was draperies I went through.

I believe it was in the opera *Andrea Chénier* that I was a soldier in the French Army during the revolution.

A nun is being led to the gallows. She is standing at the front of a small horse drawn cart.

The climatic moment comes when the curtain opens framing the nun cart and horse and four soldiers escorting her. I was standing at the front of the cart with one hand on it. My head was lowered in shame for what I had to do.

The nun slowly lifts her head, the music reaches a crescendo, the spotlight forms a halo effect around her head … and the horse shits! Splat! Splat! Splat! I danced around trying to avoid the splatter, the nun starts laughing and the curtain quickly closes!

And I was fired!

Oh well. I performed in enough operas that summer to make up my mind that opera was not my thing … but, I did get cultchur!

Horace Dodge the Third

Horace Dodge III was a legacy, meaning his father had been a member of the University of Cincinnati's Sigma Alpha Epsilon fraternity. So we were compelled to accept him as a brother. His story was that he had been kicked out of several Ivy League schools and enrolling him at UC was a last-ditch effort on the part of his parents. Grandfather Dodge (I guess the first) was one of the moneyed supporters of UC's famous co-op system.

Small in stature, he was a handsome man. One of the first things you noticed about Horace was his clothes. His grandmother evidently loved him, for she had allowed him to have an open charge account with the famous clothier, Brooks Brothers. One of his topcoats was a dark gray herringbone with a velvet collar, a Chesterfield I think they call it.

One afternoon Horace approached me. He kinda pulled me aside and quietly asked if I knew anything about Northern Kentucky. I asked him to be more specific in his question. Was he talking about gambling, after hour bars, whorehouses – what? The answer was all of the above. He made it clear that he had never been to a house of ill repute, even though he knew several girls of questionable morals. I answered in the affirmative.

The next night after dark I navigated Horace to one of the many houses in Newport. There were tall-back booths on three sides and a long bar on the other side. The "modus operandi" was you came in and sat at the bar where most of the girls were grouped. Or you could choose a booth, which offered a little more privacy. Then the girl or girls would saunter over and ask, "Buy me a drink?" or, "You looking for a little fun?" or other come-ons.

Two ladies of the evening came and sat down without the usual question. They asked us what we wanted to drink and said, "Thanks, we'll have one too." Horace and I had beer.

I can't remember what the woman had, only that it was expensive and the beer cost us a lot more than I expected – especially seeing as at the time there were about seven breweries in the immediate area. The cost did not seem to have any effect on Horace. He flashed a twenty-dollar bill and it was zapped up in a big hurry.

It was only a couple of minutes until Horace made an overture. She nodded and off they went, leaving me with the other woman. She left soon enough when she found out that I had no money.

About that time all hell broke loose. Cursing, yelling, bells ringing, screams – absolute bedlam! Someone yelled out, "It's a raid!"

With that I was out of the booth and out the front door in no time flat. I stood mingling with the crowd out on the street, looking for Horace. Many things crossed my mind. Was he arrested? Was he hurt in the stampede to clear the bar? Frantically, I looked up and down the street. A short time later on the side street I see two burly men leaving the building. They were carrying what looked to be a body. What distinguished it was that it was wrapped in a Chesterfield coat with a velvet collar. The two men heaved the body out into the middle of the street.

I had a good idea what was inside the coat. I just hoped he wasn't hurt too badly. When I got there I recognized it. It was Horace! He was laughing as he struggled to get up. "Did you hear me?" he asked, laughing.

"What happened?" I asked.

"I went up and down the halls opening doors and yelling, 'Repent you sinners!'"

All along I had been helping him to get on his feet. When he said that, I just let go. He dropped back to the pavement. I was really mad.

"You could have been killed! These people don't play around." I then stomped off to where we had parked his car (a real sporty Dodge, of course.)

Horace's attendance at U.C. did not last long after his "sermon on the mount."

Joe Martin, Union Man

Big Stone Gap was near several mining camps. No coal camp was closer than three or four miles. Stonega Coal & Coke and Virginia Coal & Iron were headquartered there.

Many of my friends' fathers were coal miners. Several had dads associated with the company. By and large our lives were influenced by the coal industry. The miners union, the United Mine Workers (UMW), was led by their firebrand leader, John L. Lewis.

World War II was raging and, even as kids, we tried to do our part. So I was upset when I learned John L. Lewis had called a strike during wartime. To me it was unpatriotic to handicap our war effort. Comparatively speaking, miners made more than any other similar laborers. I could not understand why the miners themselves agreed to strike. I guess you could classify me as a non-union man.

In the summer of 1951, my first year at the University of Cincinnati, my "co-op" job was at Heeken Can Company. I started off working on the line, packaging open-top cans in big bags. Though my fingers were cut doing this robotic job, I didn't want to wear the gloves that slowed me down. Soon after I started, a union steward tapped me on the shoulder and said he wanted to talk to me during the break. I nodded and continued working

At break time, the steward sought me out and, in a low voice, said, "Slow down! You're making the rest of us look bad." I politely told him to mind his own business and I would mind mine.

Not long after that, he accosted me while I was having lunch. "Evidently you didn't hear what I told you!" he said, pointing his finger at my chest.

"I heard you," I replied. "And you heard what I said. The way I work is my business!" I walked away.

A few days later, it was apparent that he wasn't going to let this go. "Look," he said, "You're summer hire. Your livelihood don't depend on this job. You won't be doing this for the rest of your life! Most of these people need the job year 'round. We get overtime in the summer but we can't handle layoffs if we work too hard and get ahead of schedule."

I guess I was too mad to see what he was telling me. It only reinforced my opinion of unions.

After working about a month, I was called into the main office. At first I thought I'd been reported to headquarters to explain my actions. No, that didn't make sense. After all, I was bustin' my ass for the company.

For work in the factory, I wore a pair of dungarees and a t-shirt. I was sweaty and dirty. Here I was being escorted into the head man's office – Mr. Heeken himself! Admittedly I was in a kind of state of shock. What had I done!

Mr. Heeken cordially greeted me and asked me if I wanted a coke. I told him, "No thanks," though I sure could have used one!

"Every year," Mr. Heeken began, "we look closely at our summer hires. We try to pick someone out who would like to be in position to grow with the company.

"We start training in our accounting department and move the upgraded employee around our departments. You could start tomorrow. I suggest you wear something different." I told him that I appreciated the offer and would see him tomorrow.

On the way back to U. C., the guys in my carpool could hardly believe that I was moving from the factory floor to the executive suite! When they picked me up the next morning, there I was in a sport coat and tie while they were in their grungies! I tried not to show a superior-than-thou attitude. It was a head-turning scene when I walked through the factory.

In the accounting office, I was assigned the job of posting the previous day's production. What a tedious chore! 42,396 #10 cans for Campbell's Soup; 10,481 juice cans for Minute Maid condensed orange juice; and on and on. It was evidently a banner year for Heeken Can Company and I was part of it.

At lunch time, my fellow workers couldn't wait to see why I was so dressed up. "You been kissin' ass?" asked the union steward, bitterly. We almost came to blows. My friends separated us. We were about the same size so I was not afraid to fight him. But, realistically, he was probably tougher than I was and would have whipped my ass.

The next day, I went to work again in the accounting department. Before the morning was out, I knew the can business was not for me. Near quitting time, I broke the news to Mr. Heeken. I simply told him that I had other plans for my future, like being an account executive for an advertising agency. "But we have an advertising department," he countered. I profusely thanked him and hoped the fellas from the car pool had waited for me.

The next day, when I showed up in my factory attire, the union steward gleefully said, "Ya' got fired, didn't ya'?" "Yeah," I replied and went back to work on the line.

Towards the end of July, the country had a bumper crop of vegetables, especially tomatoes. The demand for cans amazed me. The company went out into the streets and hired winos, the homeless, and other street people to keep the lines moving. My workload increased two-fold. They assigned these new hires to my line where I was to train them. I had to work my line plus runover to straighten out the slow-downs, then back to my line. We were working overtime!

In the first part of August, the foreman, Bill, called us together and told us proudly that we were ahead of schedule and he was letting go all the street folks and the summer hires.

I was shocked. I had been told we could work until the end of August. I needed the money. I raised my hand and, in a very loud voice, I said, "Bill, you promised we would have a job until the end of August."

"Well, Joe," he jokingly said, "Now you'll have some free time before school starts." I was livid.

As I was leaving, I spotted the union steward and quickly walked toward him. He clenched his fists in preparation for battle. But I just held out my hand to him and told him that I owed him an apology. He looked wary, not knowing what I was going to do next. "You were absolutely right," I admitted. "We bust our ass for the company and then they turn around and lay us off. The bastards!"

He shook my hand and said, "Well, you had to learn the hard way!"

My attitude toward unions changed when I saw the other side of the equation at a personal level. I also met Peaches and Cream. You'll learn about them later!

The Cotton Club, Peaches and Cream

The Cotton Club was a black nightclub on Eighth and Mound near downtown Cincinnati. It was noted for its after-hour jam sessions. If some well-known jazz musician was performing in the city, more than likely, he or she would end up at the Cotton Club later that night. The aficionados of good music would hear – usually through the grapevine – that so-and-so was going to sit in with the regular band.

A couple of my fraternity brothers who were musicians themselves asked if I knew anything about the club. I told them, "As long as you behaved yourself, white people were tolerated." Five of us piled into the convertible of one of my fraternity brothers one Saturday after midnight to go and listen to some great music.

When you entered, to your right was a long, horseshoe-shaped bar. To the left was the cavernous ballroom. I led the way towards the bar. The place was jammed with 95% blacks and a smattering of whites. There was no music playing – I figured the band was on a break.

I heard kind of a shrilly voice call out, "Joe, Joe!" I turned towards the sound and saw two white girls waving at me. They were sitting near the end of the horseshoe. I had to squeeze my way to them because of the narrow passageway between the bar and people sitting on stools.

As I approached, I finally recognized who they were: Peaches and Cream, the two guys who worked with me at Heeken Can! They were in drag and both looked beautiful. My friends stood together near the entrance. They watched as I made my way up to the bar.

Upon my arrival Peaches gave me a big hug. I started teasing them when this black woman said, "You leave them girls alone!" I tried to ignore her, but then she sort of pushed me and said, "I said, why don't you leave them alone!"

I told her Peaches and Cream weren't complaining and why didn't she mind her own business. Then it dawned on me – this was a man in drag too. He was wearing a low-cut dress off the shoulders. I took both hands pushed up on his/her chest and two falsies popped out! She/he screamed, catching the attention of people at the bar.

Peaches whispered, "You better get out of here." I thought it was a very good idea.

Meanwhile my friends heard the scream but did not see the falsies. They thought it best to leave too. Some of the men were getting off their barstools and were working their way towards me. I decided to bluff my way out. I grabbed a bottle of Weidemann's beer, turned around, flipped the bottle in the air, caught it (thank God!), and sauntered to the entrance. Once again, I turned towards my aggressors. This caused them to stop momentarily and I continued toward the entrance. Upon reaching the doors I ran out like a blast from a cannon. Thank God once again – my friends had gotten the car and were waiting at the front steps with the engine running. The top was down and I literally dove into the back seat, my friends pulling me into the car.

An angry group of men came out of the club only to see me wave goodbye.

The next Monday, Peaches and Cream were waiting for me to come to work. "They were going to kill you!" they both exclaimed. "They thought you had attacked that woman!"

I never went back to the Cotton Club again. I sure miss that music!

Rose la Rose

In the late 40's and the 50's Rose La Rose was "Cincinnati's Favorite" at the Gayety Theater. I believe it to be true because whenever she came to town, the place was almost full – mostly men – although a few women came to see just what it was that Rose had that they didn't have.

Several of us were sitting around in "Tummy" Taylor's room shooting the breeze when someone mentioned that Rose was in town. Jack Burns had seen her perform once and said he would give his (*censored*) to meet her.

"That's no problem, Jack," I confidently said.

"You know her?" he asked. "Nope, but I bet I can meet her and I'll take you along!"

"You will? You really will?" he said.

"I'll give her a call and set an appointment,"

I knew because of her notoriety she probably would be staying in one of Cincinnati's better hotels. Bingo! The third hotel I called rang her room for me. She answered in a very soft, feminine voice.

"Hello," Miss Rose. My name is Joe Martin and I'm a reporter for the University of Cincinnati's newspaper, *The Record*. The editor asked if I could get an interview with you for an article," I explained.

"Oh, dear," she said. "I don't have any time today, and tomorrow (Friday) will be my last performance. Could we meet say about 11:30 a.m. tomorrow morning? I must leave about noon for the theater."

"Yes, Ma'am! That would be great. I'll bring a photographer with me! See you at 11:30 a.m. in the lobby of the Netherland Plaza."

"That will be fine," she said.

I can't remember what kind of camera Jack took. It was probably a Brownie.

Right on the dot at 11:30 a.m., she sashayed across the lobby, turning heads right and left. Even though she wore heavy make-up, you could see she was a beautiful woman.

I called to her. "Miss La Rose. I'm Joe Martin." She held out her hand for me to shake. "And this is Jack Burns," who stood there like in a trance with his mouth half open.

The interview was short. I scribbled answers in a stenographer's notebook. About noon she said, "I must go," but before she left she gave me a couple of 8 x 10 promotional photos signed to me with my name. She also gave Jack a photo signed by her. His mouth was still half open and I expected him to drool anytime!

It was the best article never printed by the UC newspaper.

Uncle Ralph — The Carnie

Uncle Ralph was the black sheep of the family – shy, warm – really, a nice guy. But he achieved that mantle because he traveled with a carnival. Mom didn't speak much of Uncle Ralph, but when he would show up on our doorstep, Mom would welcome him with open arms.

I particularly enjoyed his visits because he would ask that I take some articles of clothing of his to the Royal Laundry for dry cleaning. He stressed he wanted the clothing back as soon as possible. Off I'd go in a flash to the Royal Laundry. Often I'd ask for Mr. Dixon, the manager, because I knew that if it really needed to be done quickly, he could command it. He would tell me when I could pick the garments up. Upon delivery to my uncle, I would be tipped a very generous amount of money. Usually a ten-dollar bill – or, in one case, a twenty-dollar bill! So you see why I was so anxious to be of service.

Although I desperately wanted to, Mom would never let me go visit him when he was with the carnival. She did not approve of the line of work he was in.

But while attending the University of Cincinnati, I received a phone call from Uncle Ralph. It was summertime and he said he would be arriving in Crawfordville, Indiana on a certain date. I checked my school calendar (mostly social events that I had noted) and I told him I had a weekend open. He gave me instructions and the name of the hotel and the hours he would be at "work." I went by Greyhound and arrived in town late in the afternoon. My uncle was still in his hotel room. After a dinner of hamburgers, he took me to his place of business.

His place of business consisted of a booth sandwiched between several like booths on both sides. It was about 12 by 12 feet. The front of the booth was open except for a long plank. On top of the plank set the "game." The game looked simple enough. You rolled six marbles out of a leather dice cup down an incline – which was about four-foot long – into a shallow box – about 12 inches square. The marbles bounced around until they settled into holes in the bottom of the box, which were set up in rows and were about a quarter inch apart. Between these holes were numbers – one through nine – in no particular order. It was difficult to determine which number went with which hole. Therein lay the secret of the game.

The back of the booth consisted of shelves. The lower shelves contained prizes, mostly fuzzy little animals. The larger the prize, the larger the fuzzy animal. Up above the shelves hung a big, for lack of a better word, scoreboard. Numbers, like 37 and below won a big prize; 42 got you two free throws; 48 – double your prize, etc. The object of the game was to roll the marbles then count the points, take the point count, look upon at the board in the back and determine your winnings. There was no way you could lose – or was there?

Since it was his game, Ulcle Ralph could quickly count and without looking at the board declare, "You're a winner!" He would then size up the player and quickly say, "You don't want a stuffed dog, do you?" The player would usually respond, "I don't know what I would do with it." The answer to which my uncle would say, "You seem to be lucky! If we would have been playing for money you would have won X number of dollars. Care to try your luck?" The player, almost always a man, would say something like, "Yeah, I'll try it."

Down go the marbles. Uncle Ralph quickly tallies the count while the player laboriously counts the marbles, naturally with the help of my uncle. As though he didn't know, my uncle would ask the player to see what he had won on the backboard. "Hey," he would exclaim, "I got two free throws!"

It cost 25 cents to play the game – a sum most gamblers would choose to play. Depending upon several factors, my uncle would determine whether the player was a winner or loser during the course of the game. For example, whether there was a crowd, what the weather was like, his "sizing up" the wealth of a player, the temperament of the player – was he a hothead likely to create a scene or worse still, call the cops – and whether or not he should join in on the count. Ah, there's the secret!

Most of the players assumed when my uncle counted with them he was going to cheat them in simple addition. Instead, ever so slightly he would place his finger atop a marble – and in the process, cover over a number *next* to the marble, most often the number that would decide whether the player would win or lose. The player was so engrossed in the point count, (frequently my uncle would say, "Let's count together – four and nine are thirteen; thirteen and five are 18; eighteen and nine are 27..." and so on) that the player would fail to notice the finger over the marble – thereby hiding the lower number – as my uncle only counted the number on *top* of the marble.

Often the player – or sucker or whatever you called them – would walk away losing only five or ten dollars, but not enough to create a scene. Uncle Ralph should have been a psychiatrist.

The next day he asked if I wanted to make some money. "Yes! Yes!" I was eager to replenish my meager resources.

"Here's what I want you to do." He then began to instruct me on how to be a shill.

"If I go like this," he then vigorously rubbed his face with both hands, "I want your attention. When I go like this," pulling on his ear, "I want you to move in that direction. When I put my hand on my forehead and push it back, I want you to move backwards. If I put my hand on the back of my head and nod, move to the front. When you get to the spot I'll nod my head several times. You say to him, 'I don't know how this guy stays in business, I saw him lose $50 to Luke Smith last night!' Got that?"

"Yes!" I said excitedly. I was going to get in the game!

A large crowd had gathered at the booth. The player was winning. My uncle looked nervous. He then began to rub his face.

Suddenly, it dawned on me that he was trying to get my attention! Then he rubbed his ear, after which he placed his hand at the back of his head nodding. Not once did he look at me. After I had maneuvered thru the onlookers, Ralph began nodding his head up and down.

On my right was a very ordinary looking man. He had on what we'd have called dress pants – I think a dark brown – a dress shirt – white, open at the collar – and a "man's" hat. He was standing with his arms crossed and his head was tilted. I looked him straight in the face as instructed and, in my best I don't really care voice, I said the words I was instructed to say – no variation, verbatim. The man didn't look at me, but looking at my uncle and the winning player observed, "Yeah, I don't think he knows what he's doing!"

In no time at all, the fellow had worked his way through the crowd to the booth. The happy player was leaving. My uncle looked downcast. The game began… and the player started losing right off the bat!

He continued to lose. Oh, every once in a while, he would win a game or two. You could tell he was getting sick and tired of losing. He was getting angrier and angrier. He then knew something was crooked. You sensed his frustration – it was certainly apparent to the people who had watched him losing or, better still, getting fleeced! Things were tense and I didn't know what to do to ease it.

All of a sudden, from out of nowhere, a monster of a man came through the spectators. He went directly for my uncle. Grabbing him by the lapels he pulled my uncle almost halfway across the counter. People backed away and I stood there with my mouth open and in a state of shock. "Yer cheatin' this man and I want you to let him play for nuthin' until he gets his luck back!" With that he released my uncle and pushed him back against the shelves. Good God, I'm going to see my uncle beaten up!

Uncle Ralph started smoothing out the lapels of his coat. He seemed to be trying to regain his composure. "Ok, ok, let's all settle down," he said as calmly as he could. He took the dice cup, but the big fellow grabbed his arm holding the cup.

"I'll take that!" he commanded. Then, turning to the sucker, he said, "Excuse me. Now what do you do with this?"

The gambler said, "You roll these marbles down this trough," and went on explaining how the game was played.

"Go ahead and roll," the big man commanded. When my uncle started to step in he was told in no uncertain terms that the he was to stay the hell outta the game!

After the marbles had settled into the holes, the big man bent over the marbles, turned his head and asked the player what to do next. The player watched as the big man laboriously counted the marbles. He turned and verified with the player that the count at that point was correct. Once a number was agreed on the player would look at the board and announce the results.

Three times the marbles were rolled and each time my uncle would try to protest the free play, but each time was convinced to stay out of the way. He had lost control. But all three times the poor player lost. Disgusted, he left the area and spent the rest of the night playing other games for fuzzy animals.

It was shortly after midnight. The carnival had closed down. Uncle Ralph and I were packing up the prizes, taking down the board, and putting the game away. All the stuff fit easily in my uncle's car.

Out of the corner of my eye, I saw him coming: "The Big Man." I alerted my uncle because he was heading straight towards our booth. My uncle turned to him and with a big grin, pulled out his billfold, took out a twenty dollar bill and handed it to him. "Thanks, Charlie!"

"Anytime, Gilly," and the man turned and walked away.

Like I said, my uncle should have been a psychologist! Every time I relate this story I'm reminded of the moral of this experience. Never bet a man at his own game!

Bobbie Coppens' Ass

Our sculpture classroom consisted of tall tables and backless stools. Bobbie Coppens, a good looking girl with a great figure, sat in front of Neil Davis and me. When she sat on the stool, Neil and I would draw pictures of her rear end atop the stool. At break time he and I would ask Bobbie which of us did a better rendition of her derrière.

She would explode – often ripping the papers from our hands and crumbling them up. Then she would proceed to say harsh, unladylike words to us.

One day, someone stuck their face in our classroom and announced that Mr. Nash, our instructor, would be about ten minutes late. I went up to his lectern and found he had his instructions outlined for that day's class. I took one of the pages back to my table. On the back I drew Bobbie's backside perched on the stool. Immediately she grabbed the paper and started crumpling it up. "Bobbie! Bobbie!" I cried. "That was Mr. Nash's notes for today." Horrified she began to un-crumple the page.

"Oh," she cried. "They are!" and she ran up to the lectern and started to iron out the creases with the palm of her hand. She worked frantically. Mr. Nash walked into the room and Bobbie fled to the safety of her desk.

Mr. Nash just stared at the wrinkled paper, scratched his head, and finally looked up at Bobbie and said, "Miss Coppens, what do you find so obnoxious about my notes?"

Bobbie would not talk to me for the rest of the year.

Thanksgiving at Gook's

Among my many after-class jobs while attending the University of Cincinnati, one of the early ones was a job at the California Golf Course. A misnomer – I never understood why it was so named. Since it was very near Coney Island, I thought it would be more appropriately named Coney Island Public Golf Course.

Since I had no car, I would have to take the trolley from my fraternity house to downtown Cincinnati, where I would transfer to a bus, which ran on the hour and ended up at Coney Island. All in all, if I made good connections the trip would take just over an hour.

I worked as part of the grounds crew, which did the mowing, trimming and whatever work you would think a grounds crew would do. Since the course belonged to the city, the pay was pretty good that is to say, more than the minimum wage.

On Thanksgiving Eve I received a surprise phone call from the manager of the course asking if I would come to work on Thanksgiving Day. A water pipe had burst on one of the fairways flooding it and using up an awful lot of water. He offered to pay me double time and the cost of carfare! Yessss! The thought of make all that money really motivated me. What I didn't like was that he wanted me there at daybreak, which was at 7:00 a.m.!

I was up at 5:00 a.m., caught the trolley to downtown, found a place open that had orange juice and a donut, and boarded the Coney Island bus. Upon my arrival the manager was grateful I made it. I had worn old clothes and was confident I could find the leak in no time.

No time turned out to be all day! It was getting dark and was starting to snow when my pick struck pay dirt – or, in this case, pay mud – and water bubbled out. Eureka! I had built up quite a sweat from all the hard work.

As I waited at the course bus stop, I began to get cold, being so wet and all. But the bus soon appeared – it was pure joy to get a warm ride into the city. It was also pure joy to be paid in cash for my hard work plus my busfare and a bonus! Yet another joy was that I was going to have Thanksgiving dinner that night at Gook's College Inn Restaurant and Bar near the University – All free since I was a good patron of Gook's bar. That wasn't his real name, but everyone called him that and he didn't seem to mind.

In the downtown area where I transferred, it was well lighted. Many people who had eaten in the city were now awaiting their trolley to go home. My trolley was #61, which went by the fraternity house where I would shower and change clothes. Then I would hustle down to Gook's place. Several people were also waiting at that stop.

I had not paid any attention to how I looked. I knew my pants and shoes were crusted with mud, but I hadn't looked into a mirror. A man who was waiting there looked me up and down. "Boy," he said, "Did you leave any on the ground?" Then I realized that, not only were my shoes and pants dirty, but the rest of my clothes had mud splattered all over them.

"Not much!" I replied.

He then asked, "Are you catching 61?" I nodded my head, yes. "Are you going to U.C.?" he asked. Again I nodded yes.

He turned to the awaiting crowd and in a loud voice said "You hear all these stories about college kids wasting their parents' money – drinking and partying and the like – but here's a boy working his way through school by doing dirty work on a holiday!"

I wanted to crawl under a bus. When I dared to raise my eyes I could see the crowd was giving me approval by nodding their heads and waving the OK sign.

About then our bus arrived. I quickly boarded and headed toward the rear. The same man called out to the people already on the bus about this boy working on a holiday so he could go to college. Many of the heads turned to see who it was he was talking about. It wasn't difficult for them to spot the mud dauber.

I'm just glad he didn't see me in Gook's place later that night!

Ken Wood and the Banana Crate

It was an extremely hot and humid day in Cincinnati. Ken Wood and I were walking back to campus. Our art class in watercolors had met in Eden Park, which is a beautiful area noted for its landscape. Neither one of us owned a car, so we hoofed it back.

As we attempted to cross the street – against the light and about 30 yards away from it – we almost were hit by a trolley bus pulling into a bus loading zone.

The bus driver could only nose the bus in because a fruit truck had illegally stopped in the loading zone. Ken and I quickly jumped back to the sidewalk and started towards the crosswalk.

Ken suddenly stopped. He turned to me and motioned for me to look toward the trolley bus. There, sleeping in this jam-packed bus, was an older black man. His head rested on a post between the windows.

"Look at that!" Ken said. "Here it is a hundred degrees and that old man couldn't care less!" He turned and saw, sitting on the tailgate of the fruit truck, a banana crate – the old-fashioned kind that was made out of pressed wood, like Masonite. He looked at the crate and looked back at the man.

Ken laid down his paraphernalia we used for art class, a water pail, portfolio of watercolor paper, and a tackle box with brushes, etc. He lifted the banana crate off the tailgate. It was empty!

Smiling with that big grin of his, he went over to the contented passenger who was loudly snoring. The window was open – as were all the windows since there was no air conditioning. The bus was jammed with five o'clock workers and shoppers.

Ken gently tapped on the guy's shoulder. Holding the crate out of sight Ken said, "I've got a present for you!"

The old man opened his eyes in disbelief. "A present for me?" he said, rubbing his eyes.

"Yeah!" Ken replied. With that Ken lifted the crate and started pushing it into the window.

It was a very tight squeeze but with a great deal of effort on Ken's part he "wiggled" it in a short distance – probably about three or four inches.

The fruit truck pulled out of the loading zone. The already full bus took on more passengers and started out.

I was laughing so hard it hurt as I watched the bus disappear down McMillan Avenue – the large banana crate dangling out the window. Every once in a while the crate would jiggle.

At this point let your imagination take over. What did he say to fellow passengers? What did he do with the crate even if he succeeded in getting it inside?

Ken Wood and the Winner's Circle

Don Shuman and I were fraternity pledges and our pledge chore that day was doing the dishes. Ken Wood came into the kitchen and Don asked Ken if he was going to the Indianapolis 500. Ken said yeah, he probably would seeing as, back as far as he could remember, he had never missed one race.

Don asked Ken if he had tickets. Ken told him he didn't, but that he would get a good seat anyway. Don, whose dad was a track steward, said, "My father said all the grandstand seats are sold out."

"Don't worry, Don!" Ken confidently replied, "I'll find a good seat."

The race was held on a Saturday. Don came back from Indianapolis late that same night. I happened to run into Don and asked him if he wanted to join me for breakfast or brunch in downtown Cincinnati that morning. He agreed.

Sunday morning Don and I, after a scrumptious breakfast, were passing the office building for *The Cincinnati Enquirer*, the most widely read paper in the city. Displayed in the window was a blown-up picture of the story of the day.

The photo was of Bill Vukovich drinking milk from a bottle. His pit crew was lined up in a semi circle around him and his Indy car.

"Look there!" I exclaimed. "That looks like Ken Wood!" Don studied the picture and agreed. You could recognize Ken with that big broad grin of his a mile away.

Later that Sunday evening Ken returned. Don asked, "Did you ever get to see the race?"

"Didn't you see me?" Ken practically yelled.

"See what?' asked Don.

I was in the pit crew when Vukovich won the race!"

We were dumbfounded. "How the hell did you pull that off?" Then Ken explained:

"I went up for the time trials the day before and stood at the gate where the pit crews enter. Here came Vukovich's crew. They were wearing white coveralls and a light blue windbreaker with Vukovich written in script on the back. I didn't have any white coveralls, so I had to buy a pair, but I did have a light blue windbreaker. I had lettering classes for my architecture degree, so it was no problem for me to match the lettering style.

"The day of the race, I got to the gate very early. Sure enough, they had on the same uniform that I had copied. I tailed the last man into the gate. When we got to the pit the crew quickly noticed that I wasn't one of them. The pit crew boss started to kick me out and I pleaded with him to let me stay. I told him I would be their gofer!

"Thank goodness he relented, but he did tell me under no uncertain terms to stay the hell out of the way!"

"When Vukovich won, I went with the rest of 'em to the winner's circle!" He then displayed that wide, winner's grin!

A Trip to the Indianapolis 500

Several of my fraternity brothers were from Indianapolis. Crawley Cooper was one such brother and he invited me to spend the weekend at his house. The plan was for his girlfriend to fix me up with a date. Since I had never seen the "Naptown 500" as it was called, I gladly accepted.

My date was a cute coed. We and several of Crawley's friends and his girlfriends' friends went as a group. We settled on a spot in the infield. We spread out blankets and opened picnic baskets for sandwiches, fried chicken, cold sodas, and beer. We were ready to party.

My date was not very tall – about five-foot-three or so – and she was getting exasperated because she was having hard time finding a spot near the guardrails to see the race.

I looked across the track at the grandstand. It was packed. At the base of the stands there were openings under the structure. I suggested to my date that we go investigate. She had no idea what we were going to do!

Looking around at the back of the stands, I found there were several openings between the concrete pylons that supported the structure. I took her hand and said, "Let's go!"

"Go where?" she asked.

"Just follow me," I replied. After glancing around to see who all was where, we ducked into an opening. It was dark, but we could see a slit of light at the wall of the track. We practically duck-waddled towards the light. Oh, yeah, I forgot to mention – it was muddy.

My date began to get very unhappy. "Where are you taking me?" she demanded.

"You wanted to get closer to the track and that's what we're gonna do!" I answered.

Finally, we reached the wall. Right in front of us was the track! The cars zoomed by us and the noise was ear splitting. We stood up and I glanced around to see where we were.

Policemen on stanchions just a foot or so from the stands spotted us. They looked at us with great surprise. Then they started yelling and motioning for us to get back and out from under the stands. We obliged and duck-waddled back to the rear of the stands. A group of security people met us.

I lamely explained why we did what we did. They bought it, but did escort us back to the infield and our group.

We were both muddy and had cobwebs dangling from us. I looked over at my date. I fully expected her to start yelling at me. All of a sudden she started laughing and excitedly told the group what we had experienced.

Personally, I was glad we did it. At least I got to see a racecar doing more than 190 miles per hour and reach out and almost touch it!

A postscript to this story: The famous Indy racer, Bill Vukovich was leading the pack. I was standing at the rail when his car came off the straightaway of the track and into the turn. I could scarce believe my eyes when his car climbed the wall, flipped over several times, and came to rest upside down. Flames shot out of the cockpit. He was burned alive. A sad note to a fun day.

Colonel Sanders' Country Ham

When I was going to and from the University of Cincinnati in the fifties, I would make it a point to stop in Corbin, Kentucky. Now, I do love country ham – I'd better qualify that – only if it's done right and not so salty you can hardly eat it.

There was a restaurant in Corbin called Sanders'. There I would always order the country ham sandwich. Oh, was it delicious! Many times, the owner – an old man with a goatee – would stop by and ask me if I ever tried his chicken. He said it was fried a "special way." Now I like fried chicken, but I liked his country ham more.

In 1962, Sonia and I were visiting our friends, the Yearlings, in Columbus, Ohio. Joe Yearling's father came to their apartment carrying a cardboard box containing fried chicken. He greeted us and said he had been to a meeting with some other businessmen about buying a fried chicken franchise for Ohio, Indiana, and Illinois. He asked us to try some.

"This is delicious!" I said.

"The man said his name was Colonel Sanders and he had a restaurant in your part of the country, Joe."

"Sanders' Restaurant in Corbin, Kentucky." I said.

"Yeah, that's it," he answered. "He said he had a 'special way' of cooking it." I then asked Joe's father if he liked the taste of the chicken.

"No, it's too spicy for me," he replied. "Not only did I think it was too spicy, but several of the other fellows did too. So we voted not to negotiate the deal any further!"

Next time I'm in Corbin I'm going to Sanders' restaurant and get me some Southern fried chicken done a "special way!"

Our First Christmas

Every newly married couple has to figure out how to blend two sets of family traditions into one. My new bride, Sonia, and I were no exception. Sonia's family celebrates Christmas a little bit differently than what I'm used to doing. They open presents Christmas Eve and Santa's gifts are opened the next morning, whereas our family didn't open anything until Christmas morning.

But before I get into telling about our first Christmas together, let me digress here for a moment to tell you about our first Christmas tree. We wanted to do something special – but something that fit within our newlywed budget, which wasn't much.

Our apartment walls were painted a dark green. A nice color, but definitely on the dark side, like a deep forest green. I had an idea. I wouldn't, as they did many years ago, go out and cut down a fir or some other type of fir like Norfolk pine or spruce – you know, a traditional tree. My idea was different. Instead, I cut down a sapling and brought it home. I attached the sapling's trunk to the corner of the living room and it went from the floor to the ceiling. I grafted in limbs to make it look symmetrical. I painted the whole tree white so you couldn't tell that the limbs were attached by finishing nails and glue. Then I took a spray can of imitation snow and sprayed it on the extended limbs. I took some flat paper stars that I had painted gold and attached them to the ceiling with rubber cement. From the stars, I used thread to attach plain gold ornaments of different size and sprayed artificial snow on their tops. At the bottom of the tree, a cotton base cloth went around the stand. This too got an artificial snow treatment. Boy, if it didn't look good! To add to the Christmas spirit, I cut a stencil with the word NOËL done in a modified German style lettering. There again I sprayed artificial snow into the openings. The contrast between the word and the walls was fantastic. It was really beautiful.

Now for the problem.

Sonia's parents, her grandmother, her sister Susan, her brother, Russell, and Russell's wife, Hedy, were all invited over Christmas Eve to exchange gifts – and, to my chagrin, to open them! Sonia and I had discussed this several days before their arrival and I reluctantly agreed to open presents that night.

Being the smart aleck I am, I got Sonia a cheap – and I mean cheap – jewelry box. It stood about 24 inches tall, 16 inches wide and 24 inches deep. It was covered with a hideous lime green imitation leather cover. The whole thing was made of cardboard. I had the store gift wrap it. It looked real classy – from the outside anyway.

The folks were there when Sonia took her present from under the tree. All eyes were upon her.

Well, the poor girl, when she tore away the beautiful wrapping, there it was in all its hideous grandeur. No one knew what to say – kinda like they were stunned. Sonia managed to utter, "Thank you, honey!" But she couldn't hide her disappointment.

As the giver, I was beaming. "It's got three drawers! And it will fit right in with our chest of drawers!" Sonia just nodded.

I arose early the next morning and went out to the trunk of our car to get the real presents – a blouse, a skirt, some jewelry, a pair of shoes, etc. These I put on the tree and at the base of the tree. I started fixing breakfast when Sonia sleepily came directly from the bedroom into the kitchen. Sonia was not a morning person, but managed to say a "Good morning, honey! Merry Christmas."

I gave her a hug and took her by the hand into the living room. She stood there not knowing what she was seeing, perplexed. "See, Sonia? Santa Claus came to see you! By the way, Sonia, we Martins always celebrate Christmas on Christmas Day."

The Sigma Chi Dance

Being cheap and all, I was trying to think of something to take Sonia to that would be nice and impressive but break the bank. Then I found out that the Sigma Chis were having a big shindig in the Starlight Room of the Gibson Hotel in downtown Cincinnati. I searched our fraternity bulletin board for an invitation. Not finding one, I went to see the president of the Sigma Chi chapter at U.C. "Hey, Bob," I yelled out when I spotted him on campus. "We didn't get a courtesy invitation to your big dance at the Gibson Hotel!"

Usually every fraternity invited two couples from each of the Greek frats as a courtesy. "Oh, no, Joe. Not this one," he said. "We're hosting the national convention for Sigma Chi. Delegates from all the chapters will be attending. I don't even know if all our own people will be able to go because the Starlight Room will only hold so many."

"But if I were to get in would you kick me out?" I asked.

"Joe, we're charging ten bucks a couple – in advance – and we're giving each girl an orchid corsage, so we would quickly know that you didn't have a ticket. Also, we're going to have security at each entrance, so your chances of getting in are slim to none."

"But," I countered, "If we could get in, would you kick us out?"

"Alright," he sighed with resignation. "But don't be embarrassed when you get stopped at the door."

Now there was the challenge!

First I called Sonia to see if she would be available that evening. Sonia did not have another date that night. Hurray! Second, I thought I better case the Gibson Hotel to see where the entrances to the Starlight Room were. The Starlight Room was a huge area with a kitchen at the south side and two great panoramic views of the city and Ohio River from two other sides. I found three doors into the kitchen and two doors for waiters from the kitchen that went out into the ballroom. Great possibility! The orchid was no problem. Since I worked for Klein's Department Store (a ladies store) in the display department, I knew we had plastic orchids. I wouldn't even have to buy a corsage! Everything had fallen into place! However, one thing remained: I hadn't been completely honest with Sonia.

Sonia looked beautiful in the formal. My heart was pounding. I took the plastic orchid out of the paper bag, but I had forgotten to tie a ribbon around it. And there was no way to fasten the darn thing to her gown. Oh, damn! Her mother was laughing and Sonia looked puzzled. Eventually, though, we got the flower affixed to her gown.

When we arrived at the Gibson Hotel, I ushered Sonia straight into the bar. "Can't we get a drink in the ballroom?" she asked. At that time I figured I had some more explaining to do.

"I gotta tell you something, Sonia." My mind going a thousand miles a minute. "You see, we weren't exactly invited to this event." I went on to describe how I tried unsuccessfully to finagle an invitation but this was the Sigma Chi's national convention. The nationally famous Ralph Marterie band was playing. I told her how I had made an arrangement with the local chapter president that we wouldn't get kicked out... that is, if we could get into the room without being discovered.

Now Sonia was getting mad. "I'm not going to be embarrassed by your shenanigans!" She said emphatically.

"Just give me a chance," I pleaded. After a drink she calmed down a little and after I begged and begged, she finally agreed.

We took the elevator two floors down from the ballroom. Since I had previously walked the floors, I knew the fire escape stairs that would lead us directly into the kitchen. Upon entering the kitchen, several of the employees looked at us inquisitively. My response: "Boy it sure is hot in there! We had to get some air. Which way do we go to get into the ballroom?" The staff was most accommodating.

The Marterie band was playing a slow dance tune characteristic of the '40s. Sonia and I fell in to the rhythmic swaying of the music. Sonia had her face buried into my shoulder – too afraid to look up and possibly be discovered as a crasher.

Bob did see us. He said, "I thought you must be kidding!"

Sonia had had enough! I tried to convince her that we weren't being asked to leave but she would not tolerate anymore of it. Personally, I think it was the plastic orchid that got to her!

The Brakenwoods Lane Beaver Shooting Society

Our first apartment in Cincinnati after marriage was a one-bedroom, one-bath place with a small kitchen and a recessed dinette room. There were four apartments, all with the same floor plan, in a two-story building – two apartments sat above the two ground floor apartments.

An identical building sat on either side of us. Beside our Pullman kitchen, about ten feet away, was the kitchen of the other building. The Coxes lived there.

Sonia and I were both working, so we shared the chores at home. I washed the dishes. Oftentimes, when it was warm, Judy Cox (Bruce was a male chauvinist and didn't do dishes!) and I did dishes and we would chat through the open windows.

Across the hall from us lived the bachelors – Ally Joe and Carly Gene (Alan Krantz and his roommate Carl). I don't know why we gave them such nicknames.

Above us lived two newlyweds. I don't recollect their names.

One warm night, the guys and I were sitting out on the front stoop. Bruce was relating how the two girls who lived above him seemed to be entertaining different guys at all hours. The newlywed piped in and said, "You know when they come home they always take their clothes off and parade around naked. They don't even pull their blinds!"

That statement got our attention! We five began making our plans for show time. Fortunately, all of us guys got home before our wives did – except, of course, for the bachelors who didn't seem to have steady jobs.

Here was the plan: When the girls got home, the upstairs guy would check the scenery. If the show was about to start, he would stomp on the floor three times loudly. Then, I would call Bruce who would come running over and meet me in the hallway. In the meantime, I would pound on the bachelors' door. We then would go "en masse" to the apartment above.

We weren't disappointed. I know these girls knew but didn't seem to care and the display of female flesh went on.

That is, until one day when I arrived home at my usual time. I was changing out of my work clothes and was down to putting on my slacks when there was loud, quick pounding from above. Something really must be happening! After calling Bruce, I ran over to Alley Joe and Carly Gene's apartment and said that there must be something really exciting going on.

I forgot to mention that I had not zipped up my fly – only a button held up the pants – and from the waist up I was naked.

We burst into the room. The newlyweds were hugging each other. I mumbled something like, "I thought you were in trouble with all that pounding on the floor!" A feeble excuse, but the best one I could make up at that time.

It turned out that he was tickling her and she started jumping up and down. We sheepishly excused ourselves and slunk back to our respective apartments.

His wife was astonished that all of us would come to her rescue. Then her wimp husband confessed. Boy, was she mad! So of course she told our wives. You can easily figure out that the Brackenwoods Lane Beaver Shooting Society was no more... back to *Playboy*!

Part 3

Adventures in the Military

After graduating from UC in 1956, Dad began his full-time service in the US Air Force, beginning with pilot training in Texas and Florida. He and Mom were stationed in some interesting places and had a daughter, Melissa, and a son, me, along the way. In many ways, life in the military suited the Martins just fine.

But putting a person like my father in a hierarchical structure like the military was bound to cause some problems. As we've already seen, Dad had a penchant for finding himself in the middle of mischief. At the same time, he didn't have a lot of tolerance for incompetent leadership. Though he had many superiors whom he respected greatly, it seemed that the occasional run-in with narrow-minded individuals inevitably led to flying sparks. His military career was bound to come to an end at some point – it was all a matter of time. It sure made for some great material though...

Andrew J. Hodges – Bull Rider

While in San Antonio for pre-flight training, Sonia and I decided to avail ourselves of the local events. We learned that there was going to be a first class rodeo in Bandero, Texas, the "Cowboy Capital of the World." We had never seen a rodeo, so a whole bunch of us from the base decided to go.

At the rodeo sitting beside us was Andrew J. Hodges from New York City. Andy was reading the program and he turned to me and said, "Look at this, Joe. If you stay on a bull for eight seconds you could win a hundred bucks!"

"Sure, Andy," I agreed. "But I'll bet that's the longest eight seconds of your life!"

"Come on, Joe!" "One, two," and he started counting out to eight.

Andy disappeared. We hadn't really noticed because we were up and down getting beer and such. When all of the sudden, a voice blares out over the public address system, "And riding number eight – Dynamite – Andrew J. Hodges!"

"That's Andy!" I exclaimed. And all eyes were focused on the chute. The chute opens and a body that was airborne comes bursting out. Then the bull came out minus one rider!

The airborne body hit the ground. Several of us jumped down from the stands and ran to the back of the chutes. There was Andy still dusting himself off. "How'd I do?" he asked.

"I hate to break it to you, Andy, but the bull won," I replied.

Andy snorted, "That damn event cost me $10 to enter!"

So You Wanna Learn to Scuba Dive!

Basic pilot training was at Bartow Air Base. Several of us budding aviators lived in Winter Haven, Florida just a few miles away. Most of us in the apartment complex were newly married and so the wives were not so lonely.

The u-shaped complex featured a swimming pool in the middle. Early on a Saturday morning, I decided to go for a swim.

I was enjoying the coolness of the water when I heard a voice greeting me with "Good morning!"

"Good morning!" I replied. He was a larger-than-life, big man – barrel chest, large biceps, and a mustache. He wore a DI (Drill Instructor's) hat with a perfectly flat brim. This sun-tanned giant was carrying what I recognized to be scuba diving equipment – enough for two.

"Wanna learn to scuba dive?" he asked. "I want to go over to Tampa to dive, but in unknown waters I was taught never to go alone." He went on, "I trained with the Navy SEALS. You've heard of them?" I nodded my head. "I'm a Marine scuba diver assigned to the Navy."

"Yeah!" I said. "Sounds great! I've always thought about learning!"

"First thing I want you to do is to lie down on the bottom of the pool at the four foot level," and his instructions began.

"Spit into the face mask," he ordered. "Take your finger and rub it around the glass."

"Okay," I did that and donned the mask.

He inserted the mouthpiece for me. "Start breathing naturally." And I did.

Let me say this! Scuba diving is the most unnatural thing I have ever tried to do. The one exception to that statement is golf. I never could get the proper swing to the game. But that's another story…

There I was on the bottom trying to breathe naturally! All of a sudden, something comes crashing down on my back. The mouthpiece flies out of my mouth and I suck in water. After struggling to stand up, I lay on the pool's edge coughing and vomiting. I couldn't speak and was gasping for air.

After about six of seven minutes I was able to speak the words, "What happened?"

"I jumped on your back!" he calmly explained. "That's a SEAL training tactic to show you what happens if you suddenly lose your mouthpiece. You never know what happens underwater unless you've tried it!"

"You *what?*" I cried out gasping for breath. I struggled to get the tank off my back and once I had it in front of me, I threw it at him. With a surprised look, he caught the tank in his gut.

"You son of a bitch!" I yelled. "You damn near drowned me!" By that time I didn't care how big he was. If he had touched me, I'd have killed him!

I can't remember his response; I didn't care anyway. Now I have a good idea of what it feels like when you are drowning.

That was back in 1957. In 1998, Sonia and I were vacationing in Australia. There we had an opportunity to scuba dive out on the Great Barrier Reef. Sonia talked me into trying it again. I did, but salt water seeped through my mask and went up my nose. That was it! No more! I thanked the instructor for the brief encounter and waded ashore.

Then in 2001, Sonia and I took a cruise that started in the Caribbean, went through the Panama Canal and ended in Costa Rica. The day before we were to leave the ship for home, I attended a lecture. I got there late and the speaker had already started. He was talking about working with Mel Fisher, the famous deep-sea treasure hunter.

When I looked at the speaker, he seemed familiar to me. Years before, Sonia and I toured the *Three Master*, the treasure hunting ship owned by Mel Fisher in Key West. We even invested $1,000 in his next adventure to find the gold-laden Spanish galleon. On his ship was his museum of artifacts of his collection from sunken ships.

After staring at the speaker for the longest time, something kept eating at me. He wore a full beard and had a full head of long hair that was gray. Suddenly, it came to me… this was the son of a bitch who nearly drowned me 40 years before!

When he finished he quickly left the room. I damn near crawled over people to get to him. He was surrounded by people wanting his autograph. I just barged in and asked him, "Were you ever in Winter Haven, Florida in the late '50s?"

He answered with a snarl. "I grew up in Florida so I've been there many times." He turned and quickly walked out of the room. Sonia was waiting for me so I didn't chase him down.

The next day groups with special colored baggage tags were grouped together by colors to disembark in an orderly fashion. Glancing around the room, I saw him. Working my way through the group. I finally stood face to face with him. "Were you a Marine SEAL?" I demanded

"Yeah," he said, expressionless.

"In 1957 you nearly drowned me supposedly training me to scuba dive!" I said looking him straight in the eye. He still was a big man, but he had put on some weight.

He did say he was sorry, but that's the way SEALS were trained. I can't remember exactly what my reply was. Probably "Bullshit!"

Oh, yes – Mel Fisher's stock was declared worthless. Turns out he was a big con artist!

Pilot Training

I guess it was the influence of my Uncle Charles that made me want to learn to fly. In my youth, he owned a PT-17 Stearman – the basic trainer used during WWII. He would fly it into Big Stone Gap and take me for rides. He would do aileron rolls, stalls, lazy eight turns – all types of aerobatics. And I was hooked.

So it was natural that I should enroll in Air Force Reserve Officers' Training Corps (ROTC) while in college. After graduating from the University of Cincinnati, I awaited orders to go to flying school.

Once I had completed the preliminary ground school training, I was sent to Bartow, Florida. The basic trainer there was the T-34 Mentor; the next step was a T-28, a more powerful airplane.

The T-34 was a joy to fly! It had all the instrumentation to night fly – that is, navigate by instruments only – retractable landing gear, low wing – a small but manageable airplane.

We were divided into groups of four. This enabled our flight instructor to give us each about an hour in the air.

My instructor's name was Mr. Reed. From the beginning, he was a "yeller." I didn't like that method of instruction. Once we were on the intercom, he would yell out, "Get that nose higher! More airspeed! Make that clearing turn!" And on and on and on...

But I was going to learn to fly despite him. I've got to say, my problems were not all his fault. In college I won the Professor Alienation Award several times.

For example, when you take off, you make clearing turns – first to the left, then turn to the right – and continue climbing out. The wings create pretty big blind spots, so it's easy to see why they do this for safety. On one occasion, he yelled out, "You didn't make that clearing turn right! You gotta look before you turn!"

We went around and landed and then took off again. It's called a "touch-and-go." This time, before I made my clearing turn, I stuck my head out of the open canopy. The wind caught my headphones and off they came. He landed the plane. Once we were on the ground and he had my attention, he said some rather unkind things!

It seems that I developed something of a reputation. My fellow students would come up to me after my scheduled hour. They all wanted to know if I had done anything to piss Mr. Reed off!

It had to happen. Mr. Reed and I were on a collision course.

We were about 5,000 feet above the ground when he roared over the mike, "Show me a landing characteristic stall!"

Let me pause here and explain what kind of stall he was talking about. During a landing procedure, you "trim" the aircraft. That is, you adjust the tabs on the ailerons to keep the nose up and you adjust the propeller torque by turning the wheel to compensate for the propeller's spin, which will tend to pull the airplane to the left.

In order to land, you have to pull back on the engine throttle and adjust the trim. The aircraft will then settle onto the runway. The stall occurs when you apply power by pushing the throttle forward. This can happen during a landing when the tower operator calls out "Go around!" – or abort the landing – and you quickly push the throttle forward. The nose lifts up and the airplane turns sharply to the left. When the tower orders this, you'd better turn the trim wheels to compensate for the added power – and fast!

Back to the event. As I said, we were at about 5,000 feet when Reed calls out the order. I busily adjusted the nose trim, the rotation of the propeller trim and pushed the throttle forward. I was proud of myself: I had recovered the airplane before it stalled.

"I want to feel the stall, damn it!" he loudly ordered.

We were at maybe 2,000 feet at this point in the maneuver. I busily turned the trim wheels as far as they would go; I held the stick tightly between my legs; I cut the power back.

When I had finished setting up, I called out over the intercom "Landing Characteristic Stall, sir!" With that I shoved the power forward. Then I put my hands on top of my head.

I had not realized what a crazy attitude that would put the plane into. We were literally falling out of the sky.

I calmly said over the mike, "Did you feel the stall, Mr. Reed?" Silence. Again I asked the question. No reply.

I could see the trim wheels turning. The plane was flying upside down, backwards for a while and the ground grew closer.

"Have you got it, sir?" I asked. My hands were still over my head.

Silence.

I glanced into my rear view mirror and he was busy. The plane finally leveled out. We were barely above tree tops.

Without another word, Mr. Reed landed our airplane, jumped out of the cockpit, and went running into the operations building. I was the first "up" that day. My fellow students gathered around me wanting to know what I had done to Mr. Reed.

I was describing my landing characteristic stall maneuvers when the head instructor approached our group.

"I don't know what to tell you guys," he said scratching his head. "Mr. Reed came through operations, got into his car and left."

The head instructor looked up at me and asked "What did you do today, Joe?"

I thought it best to keep my mouth shut.

Two days later, I was ordered to meet a flight evaluation board. It wasn't much of a meeting. They had already made up their collective minds. "I was a danger to myself and everyone else in the sky."

My flying days were over. When I got home, I cried. But Sonia said, "Thank you, Lord!" I figured I saved the Air Force an airplane and me a life. An even trade.

Holloman

Though not included in this collection, Dad tells a great story of how he once wrote a telegram to the Pentagon and somehow convinced them not to send him to a particularly undesirable post after he washed out of pilot training. To everyone's surprise, the tactic worked; he and Mom were instead sent to Holloman AFB near Alamogordo, New Mexico in 1957. They drove for miles over hypnotically straight roads until they arrive at a place that seemed like next to nothing. Their hearts sank as they grew to believe that this was a form of punishment, not redemption. It turned out to be their favorite place among the many interesting assignments he received while serving in the Air Force.

How to Eat Jalapeños

We arrived at Holloman Air Force Base in 1957 on a Saturday in August. Sunday morning we decided to venture out and have brunch at the Officers' Club.

It was a bright, sunny day. We found the Club. I don't know what I expected, but I sure expected something better. The Club was a one-story WWII wooden building painted white.

Upon entering from the sunshine, we had a hard time adjusting our eyes to the darkness of the Club. After about two or three minutes, my eyes could make out a man behind the bar asleep with his head cradled in one arm.

Then I saw a hand waving. As we made our way I began to see a stout person in a flowery tropical shirt and Bermuda shorts. He was the only customer in the place.

With Sonia beside me, I said "Sir, I'm Lt. Martin and this is my wife, Sonia."

"Sit down!" he commanded me.

"May I ask who you are?"

"Paul Eickenberg."

"Sir, what is your rank?" I asked, not knowing protocol, but not taking a chance.

"A captain, if you must know! Now sit down!"

Sitting on the table was a #10 can of peppers of a type I did not recognize, a small can of tuna fish, a box of Zesta saltines, and a half-empty pitcher of beer.

"Ever eaten a jalapeño pepper before?" he asked.

"No, sir," I replied. Sonia shook her head no.

"Well, you're in for a treat!" He then proceeded to reach into the big can, pull out a jalapeño, tear off the stem, split it open and, using his finger, push out the innards of the pepper. After stuffing the pepper with tuna fish, he closed the two halves and stuck them between two crackers.

The first, he handed to me and said, "Enjoy!" He then made a second one for Sonia.

Once it was in my mouth – what a great taste! Then I swallowed. A burning sensation caused me to grab for something to drink.

Capt. Eickenberg realized there were no glasses other than his and woke the bartender for two more glasses and more beer. I damn near drank the whole glass in one swallow.

Sonia was smarter than me. She just nibbled the cracker sandwich and realized it was too hot for her to eat.

Our beautiful New Mexican afternoon was wasted because Capt. Eickenberg and I ate that whole #10 can of jalapeños!

I must admit, though, he won me over in the end; jalapeños became one of my favorite foods.

A Closer Look at Air Force One

My boss, Major General Daniel E. Hooks, had been invited by General Bernard Schriever to be a guest at the retirement ceremonies for Air Force Chief of Staff, Colonel Thomas White. I accompanied Gen. Hooks as his aide-de-camp to Andrews AFB in Maryland where the ceremonies were to be held.

Upon our arrival, I saw General Schriever's aide running around like a chicken with his head cut off. "What's the matter?" I asked.

"I've got all these Generals and all these staff cars, but I don't have enough drivers with a government driver's license!"

"Hey, I can help, I said. I have a government license!"

He rounds up five generals and points out a staff car for me to drive. One good thing – at the ceremonies I was able to sit near the generals, although not in the VIP section. The retirement program was excellent, with a fly-by highlight of various aircraft that were currently in the Air Force inventory.

After the ceremony, one of the generals observed the traffic jam of people trying to leave. "Don't worry, generals," I said confidently. "I know a shortcut across Andrews."

On the way one of the generals spoke out. "Look, there is the President's new airplane!" he said excitedly. Upon hearing that, I wheeled the car around towards the modified Boeing 707 and stopped the car under the wing. What a beautiful airplane! We all got out of the car, not paying attention to what was behind us.

"Halt, sirs!" a voice roared behind us. We turned and faced several air policemen with weapons drawn. We were ordered to "spread eagle" ourselves around the car. While we were being frisked, a general beside me said, "I know one lieutenant who's not going to make captain!"

Dr. Theodore von Kármán

It was a terrible embarrassment to the United States when, in October of 1957, the Russians launched Sputnik I, the first space satellite. The US Department of Defense quickly called for a Scientific Symposium to be held. It would take place at Cloudcroft, New Mexico, about 25 miles from Holloman AFB, near Alamogordo – a location that wouldn't attract attention.

The Symposium was to be chaired by the world famous aeronautical scientist, Dr. Theodore von Kármán, one of the best minds available. Among other things, he helped develop the world's largest rocket corporation, the Aerojet-General Corp.

Included in the symposium were rocket scientists and aerodynamicists – a "who's who" among the experts involved in our so-called "space" program.

The Russians had beaten us to space. Oh, we had tried. The Navy had the Vanguard; the Army was still fooling around with the German V-2 rocket; the Air Force was trying to push the solid propellant workhorse rocket, the Aerobee, to go into the beyond. Unfortunately, they all fizzled before making it into orbit.

At that time, I was aide-de-camp to Major General Daniel E. Hooks, Commander of the Air Force Missile Development Center at Holloman AFB, located next to the Army's White Sands Missile range.

Just a month after the Sputnik launch, Gen. Hooks called me into his office and told me, in secret, about the Symposium. He wanted me to go to New York City's LaGuardia Airport and meet Dr. von Kármán who would be flying in from Italy. He had arranged for his personal C-54, a four-engine passenger plane, to pick up the eminent scientist. So it was to be two pilots, a navigator, a crew chief and me.

Before we took off, Dr. Millsaps, our chief scientist at Holloman, pulled me aside and thrust a wad of money in my hand. He hurriedly whispered that there might be a slight problem. Dr. von Kármán might be bringing his mistress! In that event, I was to use the money to buy a plane ticket for her. Dr. von Kármán had orders permitting him to fly in a military aircraft. She didn't.

Our C-54 landed at LaGuardia in plenty of time to meet von Kármán's 2:00 a.m. flight. But we had not been given instructions about where to park, so our pilot taxied up into a vacant TWA spot and cut the engines. As I was getting off the aircraft, the TWA ground crew was trying to get us to move out of the spot. Our pilot told me to move as fast as I could.

I had seen many photos of Dr. von Kármán, so I had no trouble spotting him at the terminal gate. I took his baggage tickets and, when I got to the baggage carousel, was amazed at the large amount of luggage he had. I asked him if there was anyone else traveling with him. He said no. Thank goodness!

Getting a porter, trundling all that luggage, and keeping track of my VIP took more time than I had expected. Now I might have to find where our C-54 had parked. Fortunately it was still in the TWA spot and our stubborn pilot was still arguing with the TWA ground crew!

With everyone safely aboard, we flew out of LaGuardia and headed to New Mexico. The General's C-54 was equipped with seats facing each other over a table. What an opportunity – a one-on-one conversation with the great scientist!

However, the first thing he did was ask for a glass of water. Then, from a small carry-on bag, about the size of a hat box, he started taking out vials of pills. The labels showed that he had obtained them from all over the world. I can't remember how many he took, but he spent a lot of time taking them. Well, he *was* about eighty years old.

Then he settled down. Despite his age and the long flight from Italy he had just taken, he didn't want to sleep. So I decided to ask him a question about his impressions of the multiple and as yet unsuccessful space programs we had.

"Dr. von Kármán," I asked, "What do you think about the American efforts to get something into space?"

Dr. von Kármán chuckled and replied in his eastern European accent, "Efryvun knows it takes a voman nine months to haf a baby. But you Americans! You think if you get nine vemen pregnant, you haf a baby in a month!"

Refueling at Scott AFB

We made a refueling stop at Scott AFB near St. Louis at about six a.m. on Sunday morning. An Air Force major, the Aerodrome officer for that day, met us planeside. We got off the plane and headed into base operations. The major grabbed me by the elbow, dragged me aside, and demanded, "Who in the hell is that old man?"

I started to explain but was drowned out by Dr. von Kármán who kept asking "Vere iss Schmit?"

The major turned to me. "Is he talking about *General* Smith? Commander of the Airlift Command?"

"Probably so," I replied. Our plane was carrying a "Code 2", a Very Important Person. (The president is a Code 1.) It was evident that the major had not been told anything before our plane landed.

"This guy wants me to call General Smith? You gotta be crazy! Do you realize it's six in the morning?

"Well, Major," I advised, "I think it best that you make that call."

"And I tell you, Lieutenant, it's your ass if I upset the general."

Reluctantly, he made the call which went something like this: "Good morning General. This is Major So and So, Aerodrome Officer. I have a… (aside to me – what the hell is his name?) a Dr. von Kármán here in base ops. He said he'd like to see you. (a pause to listen) Yes, sir!" The major hung up.

About five minutes later, a staff car screeches to a halt in front of base ops. A person wearing an official Air Force overcoat with three stars on the epaulettes tears out of the car. He and Dr. von Kármán embrace like long lost friends. The general was wearing his bedroom slippers and had pajamas on under his coat. The major's eyes popped wide open.

This warm reunion was broken up shortly thereafter when the pilot announced that the plane was fueled and ready to take off.

We Have Liftoff!

Shortly after the symposium, the Air Force launched the Aerobee. The nose cone was filled with cesium pellets. The goal was to shoot the pellets into near space. This would be verified by all of the state-of-the-art tracking instruments on the White Sands Missile Range.

The predawn launch allowed us to see the colorful blast that propelled the pellets into near space. What a beautiful sight!

Our public information office notified the media about the successful launch. Around noon that day, a lady from California called and said she didn't know anything about space, but a bunch of pellets landed in her back yard, and she didn't like it!

The Cocktail Party

As an aide de camp you tend to get invited to a lot of parties – probably because people assume you have the ear of the General. Nice thought, but not necessarily so.

Sonia and I thought we would repay all these folks by hosting a party at our quarters on the base. We had a miniature daschund named Hilda – a real yapper. Even though we could isolate her in a bedroom, we knew she would continue to bark, a shrill sound that pierced the eardrums. We solved that by taking her to a neighbor's house.

Among the invitees was the German Chief Scientist, Dr. Gehard Eber (I vas nefer a Nazi!) whose wife was named Hilda also. She was a real chatterbox. It was bound to happen.

I was standing at the punch bowl ladling out the laced fruit punch when Dr. Eber approached me and said, "Yoseph! I haven't seen Hilda all evening!"

"Oh no," I replied. "We sent Old Loudmouth over to the neighbors. Didn't want to hear her yap all evening!"

"Vher ess my vife!" he demanded.

The people around the punch bowl began laughing. It was then I realized what a faux pas I had made.

Dr. Eber found his wife and quickly escorted her home. After that people would ask me, "Vher ess my vife!"

Senator Barry Goldwater

Around 1960, Senator Barry Goldwater was invited to speak at a "Dining-In" at Holloman AFB, New Mexico.

My boss, Major General Daniel E. Hooks, a staunch conservative, had asked the senator, famously conservative, to be his guest at this formal, black-tie event.

As Gen. Hooks' aide-de-camp, I had made arrangements for the senator's visit. He was going to be there for only one night and had to leave early the following morning, so the logistics for his VIP visit were rather simple.

We didn't know what time he would be arriving until I got a call from Base Ops that a "Code 2" (a VIP) was en route. So I hurriedly notified the motor pool that we would need the assigned staff car and driver.

When we arrived at Base Ops, the plane was in its landing pattern. The two-seat T-33 jet trainer taxied up to Base Ops. I didn't recognize the senator until the pilot took off his helmet and a shock of silver hair appeared.

Senator Goldwater was wearing an Air Force issue, dark green flying suit. His crew chief handed him a brief case. This was his luggage? Good God, wasn't he told this was a formal affair? Then he started taking off the flying suit. Underneath he was wearing a white summer tux jacket, black tux trousers, black bow tie and shiny black shoes. I was standing there with my mouth gaping open when he said, "I like to travel light."

"Yes, sir!"

I apologized on behalf of Gen. Hooks and explained that the general was unable to meet him because he was tied up in a meeting all afternoon, but that he looked forward to seeing him that evening. It was about 2:00 p.m., so I asked if there was anything on the base he would like to see. He replied that he would just as soon go to his quarters.

After seeing the senator to his VIP quarters suite, I pointed out the guest bar, explained how to make long distance calls, etc. After my short briefing, I sought to excuse myself.

"What are you doing the rest of the afternoon, Joe?" the senator asked. I replied that my job was to take care of him while he was at Holloman.

"Why don't you fix us a drink while I get out of these duds. What do you like to drink?"

"Bourbon," I said.

"Fine" he replied. "Fix us both one with a little water in mine."

"I'd better not, sir," I cautiously replied.

"Ah, hell! Nobody will know!"

So I fixed us both bourbon and water and sat down in an easy chair. I jumped to my feet when he came out of the bedroom wearing only his undershirt and boxer shorts!

"I guess I'd better get going," I stammered after gulping down my bourbon and water. I handed him a card with telephone numbers for the general and me.

"Looks like you're ready for the reception," he remarked.

"Yes, sir. I didn't know what you wanted to do, so I went ahead and dressed for the reception." As a lieutenant, I didn't own formal mess dress. I wore what was acceptable – a class "A" uniform (standard blues), a white shirt, and a black bowtie.

"Let's talk," the senator said, sitting in an easy chair.

I admit I felt very uncomfortable in this situation.

"How about fixing us each another drink while I look over my talk." He read parts of his speech to me, asking for my comments. I remember it was mostly about the threat of communism and our deterrent, the Atlas intercontinental ballistic missile program.

I really didn't find anything wrong with the speech. As a matter of fact, I thought it was very good. After that, we started chatting about different things. In anticipation of his visit to Holloman, I had checked out a small book from the base library by Goldwater entitled, I believe, *The Conscience of a Conservative*.

I must have been feeling the effects of the liquor because I boldly told the author that I had read it and said, "Frankly, I didn't understand most of it!"

Surprisingly, he said, "I didn't either!"

I explained to him how I had been a Democrat all my life and didn't know any better.

He laughed, and thus began a great conversation. After three or four drinks, I glanced at my watch. It was 5:30. The reception was at six!

"We'll make it," the senator said confidently. "Where is it?"

I told him it was at the Officers' Club and he went into the bedroom and came out a few minutes later looking sharp in his tux.

We got to the Club at about five minutes 'til six. General Hooks had been getting concerned that we had not arrived earlier. While I arranged a reception line, General Hooks eyed me curiously and whispered, "Have you two been drinking?" I just nodded my head, afraid to say anything.

A line quickly formed and I introduced the attendees to Senator Goldwater and General Hooks as they came through. It turned out to be a great Dining-In.

Later, the general told me, "I wish that I had had what you two were drinking!"

I didn't say it, but I thought, "Two drunks in a reception line are enough!"

How Big Decisions are Made

The Atlas was our first generation of Intercontinental Ballistic Missiles made during the Cold War in the early '60s. The program was to become a major deterrent to a possible future war with Russia.

Before it was ready to launch, a decision had to be made as to who would oversee its development. My boss, Major General Daniel E. Hooks, was one of the high-ranking officers who sat on a selection board, which was chaired by a four-star General.

The board met at Andrews AFB, just outside of Washington, D.C. in strict privacy and secrecy. They met in a small auditorium located in the headquarters building of the Air Force Systems Command.

The selection was down to two major generals. Somehow or another I slipped into the auditorium without being challenged. I sat quietly in the back of the darkened auditorium. The Generals were on stage. The acoustics were good.

The two finalists had remarkable credentials. Both were fast burners (promoted below the zone[*]). Both had attended one of the service academics. It was, in my mind, a very difficult decision to make because of the importance of the Atlas program.

The discussion lasted about two hours. General Kelly began his summation. What an insightful summation it was! He talked about the service records of both generals, the pros and cons of each, until he announced his decision. I didn't know which one he would choose.

He made the decision. I was witness to his rationale. I was impressed! No wonder the Secretary of the Air Force and the Air Force Chief of Staff had asked him to head the committee.

After the meeting, I met General Hooks in the hallway, "Say, Joe, would you like to have dinner with General Kelly and me at the Officers' Club?"

"Yes, sir!"

At dinner I couldn't hold back. I told General Kelly I had attended the meeting. "You did?" He acted very surprised. I explained that I kind of slipped in.

But what I really wanted to tell the general was how impressed I was with his summation, how he stressed the positive points about each candidate, and how he rationalized his findings. General Kelly cut me off.

---

[*]They received promotions at intervals that were shorter than the norm.

He said, "I can't stand that son of a bitch–" and named the general who he hadn't selected.

I had never heard rationale so explicit!

Ah-So, Wilkin-san

Ted Wilkins was the American Red Cross representative at Holloman AFB, New Mexico, just outside of Alamogordo. I don't know what his duties were, but he always seemed to be busy. He had an office in special services and, as I understand it, he had the equivalent rank of a 2nd lieutenant. Therefore, he could belong to the Officers' Club, but didn't join because of the dues.

He and his wife were in our circle of friends and they lived on base. We'd have parties at each others' houses on kind of a rotational basis. When it came to his turn you were assured of two things: One – no booze, and two – just snacks. No hamburgers or chicken cookouts. It didn't take too long for us to figure out – Ted was cheap!

That is until it came to anything Japanese. He had an overwhelming desire to be assigned to a Red Cross post in Japan. His bookshelves were crammed with books about Japan – large, colorful and expensive books about the Rising Sun. Seems he would spend whatever he could afford on anything pertaining to that country.

One day, while reading the personals section of the base paper, the *Daily Bulletin*, I saw an ad asking for a person who could teach Japanese. Ted Wilkins' name and telephone number was on the ad.

I simply couldn't resist.

After practicing my best Japanese voice, I called him. He answered the phone and our conversation went something like this:

"Misstah Wilkin-san?"

"Yes, this is Mr. Wilkins."

"My name Yamamoto."

"What can I do for you, Mr... you said Yamamoto didn't you?"

"Ah-so."

I then made a sucking in air sound. "You learnee Joponese, yes?" I asked.

"Yes, I do want to learn how to speak Japanese."

"I teachee!"

"You will teach me Japanese?"

"Ah-so!"

"How much do you charge?"

Another long sucking in breath. "I chargee un dollah owa!"

"You charge only one dollar an hour?"

"Too much, Wilkin-san?"

"No, no that's sounds fair. When can we meet?"

"Wilkins san!" Sucking in air. "Prob-rem!"

"What's the problem?"

"I workee two jobs. I workee in Tula-asa and Alamogo-do. Me teachee night."

"Where do you work in Alamogordo?"

"I numba one cookee at Des Air Matel!"

"The Desert Air Motel?"

"Ah-so!"

"Well what time can we meet?"

"Wilkinson, I off at ten clock."

"You off at ten o'clock at night?"

Another sucking sound. "Ah-so!"

"I don't know if I can meet you that late."

Sucking sound. "Fiddy cent, Wilkin-san, owa?"

"You said 50 cents an hour?"

"Ah-so."

"Can we meet *tonight* at ten o'clock? I'll meet you in the lobby."

"Okay, Wilkin-san, I teachee Japanese."

And so it went. Ted Wilkins showed up at ten that evening at the Desert Air Motel. After waiting about ten minutes, he went to the front desk and asked if Mr. Yamamoto had come out from the kitchen.

The desk clerk assured him that there was no Japanese cook there. "Could it be Hernandez or Garcia?"

Suddenly, Ted realized that he had been had. He didn't have to guess by whom!

Major General Benjamin D. Foulois (USAF Ret.)

One of the most colorful and important people I ever met was General Benjamin D. Foulois, the first Chief of Staff of the Army Air Corps. I had the distinct pleasure of meeting him at a Commanders' conference in Los Angeles. Four-Star General Bernard Schriever, Commander of the Air Force Research and Development Command, had asked General Foulois to be an honoree at the conference.

General Schriever's Aide-de-Camp asked if I would like to go see the town (L.A.) with him. So we made arrangements to meet and have dinner at the Officers' Club before hitting the town.

When I approached the table, he got up and escorted me away from the table. Out of earshot he told me that his boss told him to take care of General Foulois that evening. He further said that the General was in his late '80s and would probably be ready for bed shortly after dinner.

That's when I first met the famous general. Sitting there in the club bar was a small, baldheaded, wiry man, smoking a pipe and drinking scotch (with a small dash of water). He started telling us stories punctuated with orders of scotch. The aide and I were attempting to match him drink for drink. Little did I know he would drink us both under the table!

My boss, Major General Daniel E. Hooks, made frequent trips to Andrews Air Force Base. I accompanied him as his aide. We took one such trip a few months after I had first met General Foulois.

We had breakfast at the Officers' Club our first morning there. After finishing, General Hooks excused himself and left. Since he would be involved in conferences that I could not attend (because I had to have a "need to know"), I had time to myself.

While enjoying my third cup of coffee, I saw General Foulois. I hadn't seen him before because he was surrounded by women. They were nurses and were now leaving for duty. So I went over to the General, introduced myself and reminded him where we had met before. He remembered and reflected that I couldn't hold my liquor very well!

The general lived in the VIP quarters next to the Officers' Club. After breakfast one day, he invited me to his home. It was loaded with memorabilia! It contained so much early history of the Army Air Corps – most aviator museums would love to have their hands on it all. This was, after all, the man who was the pilot for the military's very first plane – purchased from the Wright Brothers in 1909!

And he was a great storyteller. I'm going to try to relay this one as best as I can remember it. (I sure wish I had had a tape recorder!) After one of our several after-breakfast meetings, he asked, "Lieutenant, How many hats to do you wear?"

"Well, sir, now that I'm an aide, I wear only one," I replied. "But before when I was in the Information Services I wore several. I was Editor of the base newspaper, officer in charge of community relations, Protocol Officer, base tour guide, Armed Forces Day Project Officer, and served on the board of the Officers' Club – to name most of the hats I wore."

"Well, Lieutenant," he said, lighting his pipe. "In the Philippines as a Lieutenant before World War I, I was assigned to an army garrison not too many miles from Manila. My commander was a full colonel and a very strict disciplinarian.

"One day he called me into his office. 'Lt. Foulois, we have a problem,' he sternly said. 'A doctor in Manila treated one of our solders for venereal disease! Since you're my Public Health Officer, you've got to do something about it!'

"I had enlisted in the Army and then attended West Point where I earned my degree in engineering. I knew I was the Public Health Officer, but I thought my duty was to check our water supply and deal with sanitation problems. I started to explain to him that I had no idea how to control this problem except to confine the men to their posts. Yes! That was the solution!

"I was patting myself on the back for having solved the problem so easily! 'No!' he roared. 'That is *not* a good solution. You're punishing the troops because a few misbehaved. You should have known that because you're the Morale Officer!' 'Yes, sir,' I weakly replied. 'No Foulios, we've got to think of another way,' he said. 'Foulois, we've got to fight fire with fire!' he announced. 'We'll build our own whorehouse!'

"I didn't know what to say! I was completely speechless and in a mild case of shock. But, he continued thinking out loud.

"'Since you're our Procurement Officer, I want you to go outside the gate and look around the village and pick out a spot where we can build our own!'

"I stood there flabbergasted! '...and you're the Finance Officer. I'm sure you can come up with the funds to buy the land! It should be pretty cheap. But before you do that, discuss everything with me. Also, be thinking what kind of house you'd build. Since you're the Post Engineer it shouldn't be too difficult to design and build a house with three or four small bedrooms. Get back with me as soon as you can. We've got to stop this before the problem gets bigger!'

"My head was swirling when I saluted and left his office. I had never built a whorehouse, much less thought about it!

"Outside the base confines I found a small piece of land for a very cheap price. The head of the village, I guess you would call him the Chief, helped me select it. I don't know if he really understood what we were going to do and I really didn't want to explain too much to him.

"I reported back to the Colonel, 'I've found some land and have sketched out a design for a house. I didn't want to alert any of the troops as to what we were doing, so I did it myself,' I proudly said.

"'Good, Foulois, very good!' he said as he scanned the floor plans. 'You don't have a kitchen. You know the girls will have to live there, so they will need someplace to eat!' And the Madam should have a larger, private room for her own.'

"I nodded my head in agreement, not knowing how to respond. Then he really shook me up when he said, 'We've got to find some clean girls. Not the village girls. Some really high-class whores so our fellows will not be tempted to pick up any girls from the village.'

"High-class whores? I didn't even know any low-class whores!

"The Colonel talked on, 'We'll get them from Japan. Those women really know how to treat a man and they are clean. I know a fellow officer stationed in Japan who can probably help us with this.' So, he wrote his friend a letter and marked it 'Top Secret.' After a few weeks he heard back from his friend. Yes, he had found a Madam who had a stable of three girls.

"'Foulois, since you're my Administrations Officer, I want you to cut yourself orders to go to Japan and bring them back. You'll have to take enough money to pay for three steamship fares and any essentials they may need!'

"I left the colonel dumfounded! I had secretly hired some Filipinos who began building the house. Thank goodness, they worked for little wages. It was just about completed when I set sail for Tokyo.

"I was gone for about two weeks. The girls were typical Japanese and very shy. I guess pretty, but not by my standards. They kept mostly to themselves and only a few times had I occasion to talk to the Madam, who spoke a little English and was a no-nonsense person.

"The trip was uneventful. When we arrived at the house in the village, it dawned on me that there was no food. So I gave the Madam some of my own money to buy the essentials.

"Months went by and the "house" was making money. I was able to replenish the funds that we had used to transport the girls. Once a month a doctor visited the post and checked our men and quietly went to the house to check the women for any diseases. Disease free! I was elated! Until one day the doctor reported two cases of venereal disease. I was to report to our Commander's Office at once!

"'We've got a problem, Foulois!' I had heard that before! He then told me about the two cases. 'As Public Health Officer, I want you to investigate what the hell has happened!' 'Yes, sir!'" I saluted and left for the village.

"I quickly discovered that the Madam had secretly left for Japan. She was homesick! The girls had been left to their own devices. Evidently they had not "cleaned themselves" after the act nor had they "cleaned" their customers! As a result, the VD spread.

"I reported all this to the Commander. He put his head down over his arms on his desk so he could think, then suddenly looked up. 'Foulois, have you ever run a whorehouse?'

"I could not believe his question. Surely he was jesting! He wasn't. 'I want you to take over the operation until we can find a new Madam. We'll only have it open in the evening and it closes just before 10:00 p.m. since we have a curfew.'

"'Sir,' I started to protest, 'this is not...' He cut me off. 'Lieutenant Foulois, this is an order. We must stop this disease!'

"This was undoubtedly the most embarrassing assignment of my career! Picture, if you will, an army officer sitting behind a desk in a whorehouse. Most of the soldiers would come in, see me, and make a quick exit out. They probably thought they were going to be court marshaled.

"Shortly thereafter, the Madam returned and begged to get her old job back. You can't imagine how relieved I was. The colonel was so proud of my efforts to stamp out venereal disease. He laughingly talked about a citation and a medal. How would it read? What kind of medal would be forged?

"Use your imagination!"

Korea

Some of Dad's most touching stories come from his time stationed at Kunsan Air Base in Korea from December 1962 to January 1964, shortly after the Korean War had ended. He left behind his wife and new baby daughter, Melissa, for a year as duty called.

During that time, he developed a real love and respect for the Korean people as a result and was, I believe, a true ambassador for America as he served as Public Information Officer for the base.

Hiring a Korean Housekeeper

Capt. David N. Williams, Lt. Reed Bennett, (US Army) and I were fortunate to have a choice of living in the barracks or living in a Japanese house (or "hooch" as we called it). We grabbed at the chance to share a house.

The Japanese had built our hooch in the late '30s. It was western style ranch in that it had three bedrooms, a living room dining room, kitchen and one bath on one floor. I guess about 1100-1200 square feet in all.

The previous Korean housekeeper or "house mamasan" decided not to work for us. She gave us notice, so we had about three weeks to interview for another mamasan. Dave, Reed and I got together to discuss what qualities we would look for in our new housekeeper.

Dave, our base JAG (Judge Advocate General), was a bachelor; Reed and I were married. Dave started the discussion with what he thought was a suitable list of qualifications. "I think she should speak English, know how to use cleaning tools and products, be very clean herself, and know the proper way to do laundry."

Reed and I just looked at each other. From our brief experience of living in the barracks we doubted such a woman existed in these parts. But Dave was adamant in his requirements, so Reed and I suggested he do the interviewing and selection too. To my surprise, David agreed to do so.

The next day David went to the Korean National Personnel Office. They had a long list of applicants. According to civil service regulations, you had to take the first five applicants and after talking to each, select one. Simple enough.

After reviewing the information about the applicants, David wasn't impressed. That evening in our hooch, he shared his dismay with the prospects' qualifications.

Since I knew the civilian personnel officer, I volunteered to talk to him to see if he would make any exceptions to the rules. He granted me a private meeting and laughed when I explained David's criteria for selecting a mamasan.

We made arrangements for David to come to his office after duty hours where he would show David the applicant files, which numbered over one hundred!

A thorough man, David laboriously went through each dossier until he found five prospects. We had to allow over a week before the interviews because each had to be notified by mail and also to allow enough time to respond to the date that was set.

Times and the day were set. About three days before the interviews, David came into my office with a thoroughly disgusted look on his face.

"I have to go TDY[*] to Japan!" he exclaimed. "I won't be able to do the interviews. You've gotta do them, Joe!" I really, really did not want this task, but Reed, my other housemate, was out in the boonies and who knew when he would return. So I agreed.

When the time came though, I had forgotten about the interviews! I was wearing several hats – including additional duties such as club officer – and was so absorbed in my other duties that the interviews had completely slipped my mind.

I was abruptly reminded of my agreement with David when my airman assistant, Ed, came into my office and said, "There is a beautiful Korean woman who wants to talk to you. Civilian Personnel sent her over."

"Damn!" I said under my breath. I forgot about the housekeeper interviews! "*Housekeeper?*" Ed exclaimed. "*She's* gonna be your *housekeeper*? You officers have all the luck!"

"Just hush, Ed, and send her in." Ed shook his head, opened the door and invited her into my office. My eyes almost left their sockets. She was beautiful!

Dressed in a very chic western style woman's suit, she was statuesque – I guess she was about 5 foot 7 inches tall – and very poised.

I quickly reviewed her application and found she had attended college and had a degree! She spoke English very well. When I read that she was secretary to the president of a small textile company in Kunsan City, I couldn't help but wonder why in the hell would she want to be a maid! The fact is she could make more money than her current salary. Unbelievable! I know she would regard this job as a stepping-stone to some other civil servant job. She figured she had to start somewhere.

When she left, Ed came charging into my office, "Can you believe that?" he cried out. "You *did* hire her, didn't you?"

"I don't know, Ed," I replied. "I've got three or four more to talk to today. Again Ed just shook his head.

About on hour passed and once again Ed came into my office and announced in hushed tones, "Another beauty! Where on earth did you find these girls?"

"Just send her in."

She was not as tall as the first one but well proportioned and up to date in her western style blouse and skirt. According to her application, she had a couple of years in college and worked in an office in Kunsan City. She, too, spoke English with a Korean accent.

As she sat across from me, I had to agree with Ed, she was very attractive and seemed to be very much at ease when I questioned her about her background. Like

---

[*] Temporary Duty

the first applicant, she wanted to know more about American culture and was looking for ways to get a better job.

I thanked her and walked her to the front door. After closing the door, Ed, a bachelor, jumped out of his seat and practically yelled, "Did you get her name and phone number?"

"Yeah, Ed, I've got it. No phone – you'll have to write her." "I will, I will!" he shouted as he danced around.

Later that day, Ed stuck his head in my office and announced in a low voice, "This is the most beautiful Korean girl I have ever seen." He could hardly contain himself.

She was dressed in her native costume called a chima – very colorful and beautifully embroidered. She cautiously sat on the chair across from me. Her eyes were cast down and she spoke in a low voice.

Ed was just standing there in my office doorway gazing at this beautiful creature. I interrupted his reverie when I said, "Please close the door, Ed." He looked up at me and reluctantly nodded his head.

She did speak English, though not to the degree of the first two, and answered my questions in such a quiet voice that I had to lean forward over my desk to hear her. She was enchanting.

After the interview, I walked her out. Ed was poised in my office doorway. "Captain, I've been here about three months and I have never seen such beautiful women. Where on earth did you find them?" He pleaded. "I'll tell you about it later," I answered, though I was sworn to secrecy about how David reviewed the files.

Ed was laughing when he came into the office. "Captain, there's a mamasan waiting to see you about a job," he chuckled.

Upon entering my office, she quickly glanced around as if she didn't know what to do. I pointed to a chair. Still looking unsure as to what to do, she lifted her Korean dress and backed into the chair almost as if she had never sat in a chair. She was used to "hunkering" down or sitting on her haunches.

When I started to ask her some questions she quickly cut me off. "Me washee, shiney shoes, me numba one house mamasan!" With that pronouncement she folded her arms across her chest and stared straight ahead. Looking at her application, I saw that she had been a housekeeper before for several years.

"You're hired!" With that she jumped up and waddled out of the office. Didn't even thank me!

Ed was still laughing when he came into my office. I've got to admit, it was quite a contrast to the previous three. "Where did she come from, Captain?" he questioned.

"You didn't hire *her*, did you?" he asked. I looked him in the eye and said, "She washee, she shiney shoe, she numba one mamasan!" Ed just shook his head and slowly walked out of my office.

Several days passed when David came to my office after returning from Japan. "I can't get into our hooch!" he said angrily.

"You have a key, don't you?" I replied.

"Yes, but some woman barred the door and wouldn't let me in. I tried to tell her who I was, but evidently she doesn't speak English! She's not our new housekeeper, is she?"

"She is. She washee, she shinee shoes, she numba one mamasan! And she's doing a great job. She's also keeping our hooch safe from people like yourself just walking in!"

After a long pause, David asked, "The other four didn't work out? They couldn't speak English and weren't very clean?"

"Oh, no, David. As a matter of fact, the first two were unbelievable – western clothing, spoke very good English, answered all my questions. One of them had a college degree; the other had attended college a couple of years. The third was without a doubt the most beautiful Korean woman I have ever seen! And the fifth applicant never showed up."

Ed had been eavesdropping and after I briefly described the first three interviews, he came storming in and said "Captain Williams, you would not believe these gorgeous women! Did Captain Martin tell you he chose the old mamasan?"

David was upset. I added further to his doubts about my sanity when I told him about the third applicant. When she left the office I immediately called the custodian of the Noncommissioned Officer's Club and told him about her. He hired her on the spot.

Upon hearing that, David came to the point, "Why on earth did you hire the one we've got?"

I started to be flip, but decided he needed a straight answer. "Look, David – Reed and I are married. Surely if I had selected one of the first three there could be problems. Say on one of these cold Korean mornings I wake up and hear her padding around the hooch. Maybe I would ask myself, 'I wonder if David and Reed have left the hooch?' I did not want to be even tempted."

"Damn it, Joe. I'm not here to take care of your morals!" he said. Thankfully, our mamasan did exactly what she said she would do. If we so much as dropped a sock on the floor, it was washed, pressed and folded before we even had a chance to bend over to pick it up.

Washee, shinee shoes. Numba one mamasan! Yes, sir, that was her!

Operation Christmas Tree

At one of their infrequent visits to Kunsan, the American Presbyterian missionaries at Chong Ju were treated to a dinner at the Officers' Club. Even though it was a military base, it represented America to them. Usually four or five came. All were associated with the Presbyterian Hospital there.

On one visit I asked one of one of them what he missed most about the States. Even though it was months before Christmas, he was quick to respond, "Christmas trees!"

When Japan occupied Korea before and during WWII, they took all the trees that could be of benefit to their machines or to make charcoal briquettes. All they left were barren mountains and hillsides. After the war, the Korean government made it a crime to cut down a tree without government permission. If caught, the punishment or fine would be severe. I put the answer "Christmas tree" in the back of my mind.

When it got near Christmas, the idea came to me. We had a squadron of B-57 medium bombers rotating every 14 days from Yakota Air Base in Japan to Kunsan. They flew with empty bomb bays. At the Officers' Club I asked one of the pilots whom I had come to know, "Can you get Christmas trees in Japan?" I asked.

"Sure can," he replied "You can get some of the prettiest trees you ever saw, perfectly shaped," he continued.

"How much do they cost?" I asked.

"Oh, about a dollar or a dollar and a half," he guessed.

Pressing on, I asked, "Do you think you could get about 14 trees in your bomb bay?"

He was kind of taken aback. "What the hell for?" he demanded. So I explained as pleadingly as I could what the missionaries told me about what they missed the most. With that, he chuckled and said "Why not? I just hope I don't get caught by the Commanding Officer!"

After reviewing his rotation schedule, he called me to say he would be in Kunsan three days before Christmas Eve! What more could I ask for?

The day of their scheduled arrival, I got a call from base operations. An excited voice said, "Did you order some trees from Japan?" I said I did. "You better get down to the flight line damn quick!" Then he hung up. I was puzzled about the excitement in his voice.

When I arrived at base ops I could see beyond the runway emergency vehicles with red lights flashing. Also, on the grass sat a lone B-57 tilted up by a crane. I quickly drove up in my pick up truck to the scene. The squadron commander came tearing up to me and yelled, "Are those your damned threes?"

"Yes, sir," I replied.

"Get those damn threes out of my sight!" he screamed.

I dashed over to the trees and started to load my vehicle. Thank goodness, others started helping me. Finally, I saw my friend the pilot. He was looking very sheepish. "What happened?" I asked.

"One of the trees broke loose and damaged my hydraulic system, and another three broke loose and damaged my back up system. I had to make a dead stick landing with no brakes!" he lamented. Out of the corner of my eye I saw the commander coming toward us. I couldn't think of a better time to get out of there.

Since this happened about mid morning, I figured there was still time to deliver the trees to the missionaries at Chong Ju. It was only about 40 miles by way of a narrow gravel road. I estimated it would take a couple of hours to get there, and about an hour to unload and distribute the trees, which would give me just enough time to make it back before dark. You didn't want to drive in the black of the night. I looked at the gas gauge and thought it prudent to get it completely filled since there were no gas stations en route.

At the motor pool I started pumping gas. All of a sudden the NCO of the motor pool came tearing out of the building yelling, "There's my truck! We've been looking all over the base for it! Where did you get it, Captain?"

"I stole it. But I've got to use it to go to Chong Ju to deliver my trees!" I said.

"Captain, this vehicle belongs to the bomb squad as their alert vehicle."

"What about another truck, a half ton maybe?"

"Captain, we have no other trucks. All are out for NORs (lack of parts) and are not drivable."

"Then how am I going to get these trees to the missionaries?"

"I can't answer that, sir, but you can't have this one."

The motor pool was a secured area surrounded by a tall fence with three strands of barbed wire at the top. I asked the Sergeant if I could leave my trees there. He said I could, but only on a temporary basis.

Next day I checked with the motor pool – no trucks. The following day I checked with the motor pool – no trucks. I was really in a dilemma.

The night before Christmas Eve, I happened to meet with Major Hwang, a Korean Air Force H-34 helicopter pilot. I did my best to explain my problem – how do I get the trees to the missionaries *before* Christmas so they would have time to decorate them? I'm not sure he quite understood the reason for my sense of urgency, but he was eager to help me out. "I go to Kwan Ju tomorrow to carry some documents to the Korean Army Commander there. Maybe we get trees in helicopter." What wonderful news!

Early the next morning he and his flight crew (one NCO) and I began loading the trees. We used his jeep to transport 3 or 4 trees at a time to the ramp. They completely filled the helicopter. The crew chief and I squirmed our way into the helicopter where we laid on top of the trees, all still carefully bundled. The crew chief and I had headsets on so we could hear what was going on. We made it to Kwan Ju – his stop before Chong Ju – ok, but on the return trip, Major Hkong came on the intercom and said, "We not able to land at Chong Ju. We have heavy headwinds and low on fuel." What an unfortunate development!

"Since it's on the way, can't we just hover over the compound and push the trees out?" Reluctantly, he agreed. The chief and I worked our way down both sides of the cargo area. He unhooked the strap that was attached to the netting that held the trees in the aircraft. While hovering, we started pushing and throwing the trees out. Some of the Koreans who worked at the hospital and were outside in the yard went screaming into the houses yelling, "Bombs! Bombs! Bombs!"

We barely made it back to Kunsan. The engine was sputtering, but we landed safely. A couple of weeks later, I received letters from the children of the missionaries, many of whom had not seen a real, decorated tree except in greeting cards. The missionaries themselves were completely in awe. They still talk about being bombed by trees at Christmas.

How I Became a Club Officer

How I became a club officer in one easy lesson: I was ordered to do it!

Not too long after I arrived in Korea, I was named Club Officer by Col. Thompson. The previous Club Officer was transferred rather quickly. Soon after, I began looking over the books. It was apparent that the Club was losing money. I knew next to nothing about running a club. But I could not imagine why the Officers' Club shouldn't be making a profit. We had a captive audience, four slot machines (two dime slots and two quarter slots), a package store for liquor, a dining room, and a bar. Seemed like plenty of income potential there.

I didn't want the job. When given the order to take over the operation, I protested. One of my reasons was that my primary job of being Public Information Officer was beset by problems. The previous officer had gone berserk and had to be air evacuated to the States; the office was in much disarray; and I had no Airman helper – even though the manning document had called for one information specialist.

I learned that the Officers' Club at Osan had undergone an audit and inspection because they too were losing money hand over fist. Seems that some of the waitresses would write an order and then hand the bill to the cashier after it was paid. Later on, the Club manager would destroy some of the bills and then split the money with the cashier and the waitresses while he keeping the lion's share for himself.

I tried to visualize the same thing happening at my Club – but how do you catch them doing it? I was too busy to keep an eye on all the activities at mealtime. We were losing our inventory of cigarettes, booze, and food supplies somehow too. No big robberies, but it seemed that a little bit was stolen here and there.

I almost forgot about the slot machines. They were constantly played by the rotating pilots who were on alert; they still make it to the flight line in the same amount of time it would take to get to the planes from the alert barracks.

I had to devise a plan. It had to be simple so that I could understand it and follow it too! So I asked myself – what would I steal if I were a Korean employee and worked at a place like the Club? One quick thing came to mind: cigarettes! Black market cigarettes in Kunsan City were worth good money. Korean cigarettes tasted like you-know-what!

The second thing I thought of was meat, especially steaks. The Koreans love bulgogi, which is marinated beef cooked over a dome-shaped grill that sits on a charcoal clay vase. It is delicious! But beef was very expensive there and, again, a logical thing to steal. One day I happened to see some of my employees eating in the kitchen – no problem there because they were eating their native dishes. But what struck me was their use of Tabasco hot sauce! Another item to watch.

The slot machines were another problem, but I countered that by telling my bartenders and the cashier who took in the money every night that no monies were to be taken from the machines except in the morning at 9:00 a.m. and I was the one who counted the proceeds.

The cashier's cage was located in the package store, which was also where folks bought cigarettes. I selected two brands to monitor – Winstons and Salems – by far the most popular smokes of that time.

Then the work began. I told no one what my plans were. After the Club closed, I would go back into the Club and count the number of sirloin steaks. I counted the bottles of Tabasco sauce in the supply room and on the tables. I inventoried the cigarettes – both in the cashier's cage and in the supply room.

Might sound silly, but it started paying off. I would go to our cashier – we called her "Missy" – look up at the Winstons and say, "Looks like we sold four cartons today. Let me see your inventory sheet. Hmm, what happened to one carton?"

Missy would hang her head and softly reply, "I don't know, sir!" I didn't think she was involved in the thievery, but our supply manager – him I didn't trust.

One day I offhandedly said to him, "Gimme a cigarette, Kim." Out of habit he pulled out a pack of Salem's, which had a special label on the package. "Gotcha!" I said. He looked like he was dying a thousand deaths! "Kim, I better not catch you with another pack of American serviceman's cigarettes."

I would go into the kitchen and open the freezer and count the sirloin steaks. I knew from the night before how many were there. Next, I would check with the cashier for the number of steak dinners we served that night. If one steak was not accounted for, I went into the kitchen and asked the head cook where the missing steak was. Same thing with the Tabasco sauce. The Club staff didn't know whether or not I was brilliant or had gone crazy. I would confront the head cook and say, "For every steak that is missing, you will buy one." Naturally, he was upset and would plead with me that he didn't steal it.

Gradually, things started improving. The Club got closer and closer to being in the black. But the real *coup de grace* came one night when I went back to the Club after hours.

I don't know why, but I took a different route home that night and saw a light coming from a small top window. Curious, I figured the light must be from the entertainer's dressing room behind the ballroom. With the aid of an empty wooden box, I climbed up and peered into the window.

There they were: my supply room manager, a cook (not the head cook) a waitress and my night janitor! All were dividing out loot they had accumulated.

I quickly entered to Club and went to the only entrance to the dressing room. Through the door I could hear them laughing and just having a good old time. At that point I opened the door.

You should have seen their expressions. Shocked! Caught in the act, they started pleading with me not to fire them. So, I made a bargain with them. I would write a letter of reprimand and give them a copy. I would keep a copy and, if ever I caught any of them stealing again, they would be fired and that letter and another would be given to the Korean Civilian Personnel Officer. If that happened, their chances of working on Kunsan Air Base would be slim to none.

The Club began to be very prosperous!

...And the Club Burns Down

The Airmen's Dinning Hall won the Hennessy award for being the best of its kind. Gen. Emmit "Rosie" O'Donnell himself and his staff were coming to Kunsan to present the trophy. Great news! But I could visualize that I was going to be a very busy man – coordinating news releases with our parent commander at the 510th Air Division, photo opportunities, maybe even a front page photo in the *Stars and Stripes*. The possibilities of publicizing the event seemed endless.

Then there was protocol. Since I was in charge of that catch-all duty, I began to plan out what I thought would be appropriate within the time limits of his stay. Add to that community relations: Could I invite the Mayor of Kunsan and the Governor of the province? And the list went on. We received the notice of his arrival just a week or so before and all this hinged on one thing: What did the base commander, Col. Glenn Thompson, want?

At the first staff meeting that we held on the matter, Col. Thompson revealed his thoughts on what should happen.

"We'll have the awards ceremony at the Officers' Club," he flatly stated. "Then the next morning he can tour the Airmens' Dining Hall. He'll be leaving right after that for Osan."

I damn near fell out of my seat! "The Officers' Club?" I almost shouted. "The Airmen's Dining Hall won it – why don't we have the banquet there?"

"I said we're going to have it in the Officers' Club and that's final!" he angrily said. I was not in good terms with Col. Thompson anyway. I made my pitch and thought better not to press it any further.

The next staff meeting was on a Saturday morning at 9:00 a.m. The purpose was to finalize the plans for Gen. O'Donnell's arrival. When Col. Thompson asked for comments, I blurted out that I still could not understand why the staff at the Airmen's Dining Hall was not getting more attention. Oh Lord! The volcano erupted!

"We're having the affair at the Officers' Club and that's final!" he roared. Then he added, "The steaks we've been getting at the club are lousy." On this I agreed with him. I explained to the staff that the Army controlled all the meat shipments to the many service clubs and dining halls and we were at their mercy. That wasn't good enough for the Colonel.

He turned to Col. Bill Blankenship, the operations officer, and ordered, "Get an airplane and take Captain Martin wherever he has to go and get some good sirloin steaks." He then dismissed us.

What to do next? All these other things demanding my time and now I was ordered to find the best steaks in Korea. Unbelievable! I remembered talking to the NCO club custodian once about how the Army allocated the meat. I recalled him mentioning an Army Chief Warrant Officer in Seoul who was responsible for the allocation. So I called our NCO Club and the custodian answered the phone. Great! I told him my problem.

"Captain," he calmly said, "I'd be worrying about where I would put them."

Let me pause here. We'd had been having freezer problems – some were down because we had to order the parts from the US. We couldn't simply go to Japan to find them. So I replied, "Oh, I think we got one of them working by robbing parts off the others."

"You don't get my point, sir," he said. "Your club's on fire!" Thinking this was a joke, I told him I still wanted the name of the Warrant Officer in Seoul. "Just a minute, sir. I'll have to look for it." Pretty soon he came back on the line with the name and number.

Then I started worrying that maybe he wasn't joking. My information office was next to the headquarters building. The Officers' Club was nestled in some trees across the golf course from my office. I dashed outside to see if I could see what was going on. There was a haze, but nothing discernable, or at least I couldn't see any activity. Probably a kitchen fire, which was not uncommon.

Just to be sure, I called the Club. We had two numbers – both were busy. So, I called the fire department. "Yes, sir," the lackadaisical voice responded. "We sent one truck and now we're sending more." Again, I tried to call the Club; both lines were busy. Again, I ran out the door and in the distance I could see the flashing red signal on a fire truck.

The telephone was ringing when I went back into my office. It was Col. Blankenship. "I've got our plane now, where do we go?" he asked.

"Colonel," I answered, "I've got a problem. My Club's on fire."

"Your ass will be on fire if you don't get those steaks! I'll be down to pick you up."

When he got to my office I jumped in and said, "Let's take a shortcut to the Club." "Okay," he said and he barreled on over the golf course directly to the Club.

A large gathering stood outside, mostly my employees. The firemen had ordered everyone out. Even though there was a lot of activity, it was strangely quiet.

"Kaboom!" In a flash the whole Club was engulfed in flames. There stood Col. Thompson, a cigar clenched between his teeth. Being the smart aleck I am I said, "Looks like we'll have the party at the Airmen's Dining Hall after all!" He had fire in his eyes.

"You have those steaks yet?" he yelled.

"I'm gettin' 'em, sir!" I replied. Col. Blankenship all this time had been trying to drag me away from the Colonel. He told me later that he really thought the Colonel was going to strangle me.

My Korean club manager, Kim, was standing there in a stupor. Tears were in his eyes as well as many of my employees' eyes. I assured Kim that no one would lose their jobs and that there was plenty of work to be done.

Col. Blankenship and I took off for Seoul. The flight time was just over an hour. After landing at Kimpo Air Base just outside of Seoul I made my phone call to Warrant Officer Smith. Military protocol states that you address them as "Mister." You can imagine my surprise when he answered the phone!

"Mr. Smith, this is Captain Martin. I need 24 sirloin steaks and I need the best you have."

"Well, sir, I can help you out but it's going to cost you!" he said.

"I don't care how much they cost, but they better be good!" I replied. "If I find one tough steak I'm gonna come back to Seoul and kill you. You can take that anyway you want Mr. Smith!" I said with much emphasis.

"I got your point, sir," he said. We made arrangements for them to be packed in ice and delivered to the Kimpo Officers' Club.

"By the way, sir, did you say you were from Kunsan?" he asked.

"Yes," I replied.

"Didn't your club burn down just today?" he asked.

"You're right, but I'll worry about that tomorrow!" I said, remembering Scarlet O'Hara's famous line. Word does travel fast.

We met Mr. Smith later that afternoon. The steaks were nicely packed in ice and I took out several and took a good look at them. "They're well marbled, sir, and nice and thick," he emphasized. The steaks cost $3 each, a high price for government issue.

"I'll get the plane and we'll go," said Colonel Blankenship.

"No way!" I answered. "Back in Kunsan there's nothing but trouble!"

"But, Col. Thompson..." the colonel interjected.

"Col. Thompson doesn't have any idea of the time it took to find these steaks. Let's stay all night in Seoul."

"But where?" he asked.

"Where" was a little known hotel run by the armed forces for VIPs coming to Korea. It was an out-of-the-way place that would be difficult to find, even if you had the address. I had found out about it from a Master Sergeant who ran the place and I just happened to have his number. So I called him.

To my surprise, he answered the phone. I couldn't believe I could find people on duty on such a beautiful Saturday afternoon. "Hi! This is Captain Martin, do you have room in the inn for tonight?"

"Is this the Captain Martin from Kunsan?"

"Yes," I replied.

"Didn't your club just burn down?" Again I confirmed what he'd heard. "Where are you now?"

"I'm at Kimpo."

"Sure, I've got room. In fact, I'll give you Gen. Hutchinson's room!" The General was Commander of the 310th Air Division – Col. Thompson's base. After getting the address and directions from him, we hailed a taxi and off we went.

What a neat place! Everything was downsized – not in quality but in space. It had a small dining room, and a small but well-stocked bar. I don't remember the number of rooms, but I can sure remember that VIP suite! Everything that a first class hotel could provide, these quarters could match. We had a quiet dinner (with drinks before) and since it had been such a hectic day, we went to our rooms. I don't think Col. Blankenship knew what my room looked like. If he did, he didn't say.

The next morning after a delicious breakfast, we went to check out. "No charge," said the custodian. "I figure you have so many other problems right now, it's the least I can do for you!"

The flight back was uneventful, except the Kunsan tower radioed when we were about a half hour out.

"Is Captain Martin with you?"

"Yes."

"Tell him Col. Thompson wants to see him just as soon as you land."

"Roger," replied Col. Blankenship.

We landed and the Colonel dropped me off at my hootch (the Japanese for little house). My two roommates pounded on me, "Where in the hell have you been?"

"I went to Seoul," I calmly replied.

"Did you know your club burned down?"

"Yes, I was aware of that."

"Col. Thompson has been calling here every hour," said David. The phone was ringing. David said, "It's probably for you!"

"Please answer it, David," I asked. He put his hand over the mouthpiece and handed me the phone. "It's Col. Thompson and he sounds madder than hell!"

I took the receiver and as jovial as I could sound said, "Hello, Col. Thompson. I was just about to call you." Then I held the phone out so Reed and David could hear the conversation.

Col. Thompson was pissed! Both my roommates could hear him chewing my butt out. Then, he said, "We're going to remodel the VIP hootch and turn it into the new Officers' Club!"

As unbelievable as it sounded, it did happen. Col. Faulds and his civil engineers along with some volunteers who chipped in to help began the process of converting a three bedroom house with one bath, a kitchen, a living room, and a dining room into a single large dining area with a bar. Only the bath and kitchen stayed like they were.

My job was to replenish the stuff we needed to have a large dining room and a well-stocked bar. You can well imagine what all was needed to do this because everything we had was lost in the fire. The NCO and the Airmen's Clubs both chipped in with glasses of all sizes, cloth and paper napkins, table cloths, silverware, cooking utensils – you name it, we needed it. All the things we borrowed had to be accounted for. But, with a little help from my friends, as the song goes, everything fell into place. Col. Faulds and his people really came through and shazam! – we had a club.

I can't remember who, but some clever person came up with a name for our new club: "The Bottom of the Mark," named after the famous bar atop the Mark Hopkins Hotel in San Francisco, which was called, appropriately enough, "The Top of the Mark."

About those steaks. Gen. O'Donnell and his entourage plus a few of Col. Thompson's staff enjoyed those perfect steaks. I wasn't invited. Instead, I ate at the Airmen's Dining Hall – and I relished every bite! They really deserved to win the trophy!

The Club Fire and the Aftermath

Just when I thought things might quiet down, PACAF Services, which had all the Air Force under their watchful eye, sent Col. Thompson a long letter saying that an inventory was to be taken for what had been lost. The letter was passed on to me for action.

What was left was no problem. There was nothing left. You've got to remember that I had been Club Officer for about a month before the disastrous fire. PACAF wanted a detailed list of what we lost. My Korean manager, Kim Mun Sun, had been in the job over 13 years. The supply man, I believe, had about five years at the Club, and there were others who could help out.

Let me state at the get-go: I like Koreans. They are good, hard working people who had been slapped around first by the Chinese and then the Japanese. The decades of oppression had toughened them, making them highly resilient.

So, we divided the burned down Club into areas or rooms and tried to draw a picture in our minds what was there that occupied space. For example, I remembered the bar had two coolers for beer and one cooler for soft drinks. "Picture this - me talking with Kim the bartender: "The cooler on the left hand held four cases of beer." "Oh, yes!" he would agree. Then I would counter that by saying, "But, it could have held six cases, yes?" "Oh, yes!" he would affirm. My employees would agree with anything I would say. So you can see my problem in establishing our losses.

The layout of the dining room was another story. The waitresses knew the layout of the dining room by heart, so at least that part was easy.

In the end, things went rather well (to my surprise). After all, if I was wrong, who would challenge me? We had a large insurance policy that would cover most of our losses. Hooray! Now to collect.

Collecting the Insurance Money

PACAF Special Services in Hawaii informed me the Club had a large fire insurance policy. If I remember correctly, it was about $100,000… a lot of money back then.

The policy was issued by an insurance company in Seoul. Two Englishmen ran the company. I was given the policy claim number and the insurance office telephone number. This number I tried several times, but got no answer.

I received my Commander's permission to go to Seoul and find this company since I also had their address. I arrived in Kempo Air Base, Seoul late morning and took a taxi to the address I had been given. It was a large office building and I found the name of the company on a master directory on the wall at the entrance.

Their office was on the 5th floor. After wandering down the hall I came across the number on the door. A huge sign was over the top part of the frosted glass door. The sign was in English and Korean. In bold letters it read: "This office is closed. The (names of the two Englishmen) have been arrested for treason by order of the Government of Korea."

Just my luck!

Across the hall was a Dutch Maritime Insurance Co., which I thought might have more information. The Korean secretary at the front entrance went into another office. Out came a big man – I mean big. In broken English he asked, "You vaunt (the name of the Englishmen)?"

"Yes, sir," I replied. "I have an insurance policy with them on a Club at Kunsan."

"Your Club burned down!" he bellowed and heartily laughed. I didn't see the humor, but I was amazed that he had heard about it. "They go to jail," he explained.

"Yeah, I can see the sign. But what in the hell did they do?" I continued.

"Politics!" he answered. "They gave money to the wrong man who vast running for office. Come! I help you. We go eat first."

"Ok." I nodded.

He took me to an international club, which had guards at the gate. I was really impressed with the inside. It reminded me of the staid Club of England with overstuffed chairs and an abundance of waiters attending to your every need. "Vee haf a drink, Yes?" he asked.

Since I was going to stay overnight, I said, "Yes!" I needed a drink!

After a casual wonderful meal from an English style food menu, we leisurely walked back to his office, which was nearby.

"I haf goot news for you!" after he cradled the phone. "Your insurance company vill let me handle your claim!" What a relief. Not too long after that, the claim was paid. The check had to be sent to PACAF headquarters. I really owe a debt of gratitude to the Dutchman.

Fifty Won Hill

I asked the commander of the air police, CWO Jernigan, if I could go on a night patrol in Kunsan City. The night patrol consisted of an American air policeman, a Korean air policeman, a Korean national policeman, a plain clothes Korean detective, and an interpreter.

Jernigan arranged for me to go one weekday night. The group started out at 10:00 p.m. The reason for this hour was that it was curfew time for all military personnel (both American and Korean) as well as all Korean civil servants to be off the streets.

We began with the bars. Upon entering one, we scanned the place for any of the above. The Koreans would approach an individual and demand identification. They did not ask for it in a nice way. Especially in places that were "off limits" to the folks described above.

One of the "off limits" places that were searched was 50 Won Hill, known for its prostitution at very low prices. Fifty Won was worth, say, 50¢. The roads, or paths, were not paved and since it had rained that day the paths were muddy. The benjo ditches (open sewers) ran along beside the paths. It was pitch black and everyone, except me, carried a flashlight.

A young boy about 11 or 12 ran into us as we were going up the hill, well past curfew time. We knew he was a schoolboy because he wore a black tunic, black pants and a small black cap, as did all the small school children.

He was clearly startled and frightened by having run into us. "Who are you?" the National Policeman demanded. The boy did not reply. He stood at attention and stared straight ahead. "What are you doing here?" he continued his query. Still the boy did not reply and stood stonily on the path.

The policeman slapped him hard. The youngster recoiled with pain. "I asked you your name!" Again, the boy said nothing. Again the policeman hit him, only this time harder. The policeman was angry that he could not get the boy to respond. He stood there mute.

The policeman hauled off and kicked him in the shins. The boy collapsed in pain and struggled to get up. I could not see beating the boy because he had missed curfew. I knew I didn't have the authority, but I stepped in between the policeman and the kid. "That's enough!" I said. The group was surprised that I should interfere.

The American Air Policeman whispered in my ear. "Sir, we're not supposed to get involved in their investigation!" I nodded my head. The policeman just stared at me with hatred. He stepped back from the kid and shone the flashlight in the kid's face. By this time the tears were flowing, but he would not say a word. "Oh, ha!"

cried the policeman. "You go to Ok Pong School and you are in the fifth grade. I tell your principal."

With that news the boy fell to the ground grabbed the policeman by the legs and pleaded with him not to tell his principal. He cried loudly and told the policeman that he was in 50 Won Hill visiting his mother who was a prostitute. He had forgotten the time and was on his way back home to his grandmother's when we ran into him.

After a harsh lecture, they let the boy go. He was limping as he left our group. I wonder how many American kids would be that afraid of being expelled from school.

The Sign Painter at Tae Chon Beach

It was tradition that, each year, the Club Officer took the employees of the Officers' Club, numbering about 32, to Tae Chon Beach, a lovely stretch of sand on the Yellow Sea. Half would go one weekend and half the other.

To get to the beach you'd take a ferry from Kunsan City across an inlet to Edi, a small city, catch a train to Tae Chon, and from there go by bus to the beach. All in all, it was about a three-hour trip if you made connections as planned.

We were scheduled to leave Kunsan City on the eight o'clock ferry. About five that morning, I received a call from the Air Police saying that a young GI had committed suicide at the Ariel Port. I quickly dressed to go to the scene.

Upon my arrival at the building, nothing had been removed because the base doctor had not finished examining the body. I watched as they unclenched his hand, which held a crumpled piece of paper. I had to be there because I had yet another "additional duty" – Summary Court Officer, which meant I was to investigate circumstances surrounding incidents like these.

The staff Judge Advocate finally arrived and released me to go to Tae Chon, which I had temporary duty permission to do. I quickly rushed off the base hoping to meet my club employees for the eight o'clock ferry. Unfortunately, it had just left. An hour later I caught the next ferry.

At the Edi train station, I did my best to read in Korean the next scheduled train that went to Seoul with stops along the way at places like Tae Chon. It would be another hour. Again, I just missed the train my people would be on.

In what seemed like an eternity, I finally boarded a really uncomfortable passenger car. Since I was wearing my Class A uniform, fellow travelers shared their breakfast with me. I elected to try a white, glutinous-looking bun thinking it may be a type of breakfast roll. But no, it was filled with a dark soybean mixture that was anything but sweet. I did enjoy a big juicy apple someone generously gave to me.

Our train did not arrive in Tae Chon until four that afternoon. The bus ride to the beach took about a half hour. It was jammed with vacationers and everyone had eaten lots of Kimchi, their national dish. Kimchi isn't exactly the best smelling stuff in my book.

Upon my arrival at the beach, I got off the bus eager to get a breath of fresh open air. However, the Yellow Sea at Tae Chon doesn't smell that great. With my uniform on, I was burning up.

I had no idea how big an area the beach covered – I would guess maybe a half-mile. I took my uniform blouse off, unleashed my tie, took off my shoes and socks, tied the shoes together, and started walking up the sand while scanning the beach for my people. I thought surely I would see one of them swimming.

No luck! After going north to the end of the beach, I turned around and trudged back to where I started. In front of me was a new hotel that looked like it had just been completed.

On the ground next to a hotel a sign painter laboriously was painting on a four-by-eight-foot piece of painted white plywood, lettering that said "O.B. Western Hotel" and underneath in smaller lettering "Western Style Rooms." I guessed this was to appeal to the western tourist or military people who wanted to stay at the beach.

The lettering was crudely done. In college at the University of Cincinnati, I had majored in Applied Arts. Lettering design was one of my classes.

I stood there observing his work when a voice behind me said, in broken English, "You like? You stay at my hotel?"

"Thank you." I responded. "But I'm looking for some people who have a place for me to stay!"

"I show you my hotel," he insisted.

"I'll see it later. Right now I'm looking for my people."

The sun was starting to set and I had no idea what my next move would be. Suddenly I thought: if I painted him a sign, maybe he would give me a free room!

You see, I was in a real bind. In my haste to leave Kunsan and catch the eight o'clock ferry, I had not had any time to stop by my hooch and pick up my small bag that had a change of underwear, my shaving kit, toothpaste and toothbrush, and swim trunks. Add to that, I had no money; my Korean club manager had all the funds. I only had a few dollars of Military Currency Pay (MCP) and that was no good there. The few Korean won I had went for the transportation to get here. I had a problem for sure.

I thought I would lay it on the line with the manager. I told him that I had no money. He repeated "No, money?" As an American officer, he, as most Koreans, thought I must be loaded with cash.

I tried to explain my situation and he seemed to understand. I made a bargain with him. I would finish painting the sign in exchange for a room at his hotel. He quickly agreed and shooed the painter away. He gave me a towel and I dropped to my knees and began to correct the lettering.

Pretty soon a crowd gathered. The manager beamed! He had this American officer in front of his hotel… working for him! Everyone watched as I carefully lettered the sign.

"Captain Martin!" a voice yelled out. "What are you doing?" It was my club manager. He had heard from others down the beach that this hotel manager had this American officer working for him. "We have a hotel room for you! Where have you been? When did you get here?" He was full of questions.

"Just let me finish this sign, Kim and we'll talk," I explained. It was getting dark by then and I wanted to finish my work.

"Go get our people and bring them up here to this hotel and we'll have a party!" I ordered. He turned and started to run down the beach to get the employees.

The manager of the hotel invited his employees to join us. We had a great party. It must have been because the next morning my head really ached!

Let me tell you about the room. In the center was a huge trundle bed with a bed underneath and a beautifully carved headboard. The dresser evidently came from the same set. The manager told me later that he bought both pieces from a missionary.

The bathroom was something to behold! First of all it was small. The walls, floor and ceiling were all concrete. A single galvanized water pipe came in from the outside near the ceiling. It ran parallel to the ceiling then made a "T" connection – one pipe came down to the sink, cold water only; the next T connection went to the toilet; the third went to the shower nozzle. The shower had a pan-shaped concrete basin with a drain but no curtain. The shower was fed by the same cold water pipe.

The manager was extremely pleased with his "westernized" room!

The Arial Port Suicide

The young airman I mentioned before had taken an AK-47 rifle and put it between his legs with the barrel under his chin. I was told he died instantly.

Clutched in his hand was a piece of notepaper. When the doctor pried it out of his hand and uncrumpled it, we found the reason he had taken his own life. He had fallen in love with a prostitute!

He was a good-looking kid – about 19 or 20 – and hailed from Small Town, USA. His non-commissioned supervisor was as surprised as anyone why he would take this extreme measure. He had been promoted on schedule and was a good worker – an - around airman.

Searching his room he shared with other enlisted troops, I found other love letters and poems he had written to the prostitute. I could find no notes or letters from her, only a photo of them together. It looked to be professionally done.

It was not hard to find her since she lived in a village not too far from the base. Not only that, but she was well known in Kunsan City as "Ok Pong Rose." I interviewed Rose and when I told her of the young airman's death, she appeared not to have any remorse. She didn't shed a single tear!

"Too bad," was her explanation. "I tell him I business girl. I no marry him! He come all time to my hooch" (Japanese for house). "He nice GI. I tell him all time I business girl. He no believe me!"

How I wished he had believed her.

A Trip to Osaka

Kim Houng Do became a very good friend to me. He was a major in the Korean Air Force and "volunteered" to be my interpreter. A Korean Air Force Academy graduate, he took helicopter pilot training in Texas. This history was reflected when he spoke certain English words with a definite Texas drawl.

He was engaged to a lovely Korean lady who was an accomplished musician. The piano was her forte. She lived in Kunsan City with her mother in a very nice traditional Korean house that had sliding doors and a beautiful small garden.

Her father lived in Japan. During WWII he worked for the Japanese Government. At the end of the war he left quickly for Japan leaving the family behind. Any Koreans who voluntarily worked for the Japanese were considered traitors and were *persona non grata*.

I mentioned to Kim that I was going to take a week's R & R (rest and relaxation) in Japan. "Why don't you stay with my future father-in-law?" he asked. "He lives in Osaka and since you and I are friends, he would love to meet you!"

"Oh, I couldn't impose on him like that," I replied. "Look, Joe," Kim said, "he is very wealthy and has a big house with lots of servants. He cannot come to our wedding so he will want to hear about me and his daughter."

"I don't know, Kim," I said doubtfully.

"No sweat! I will write to him today. You won't be going for a month – plenty of time to make arrangements!"

The more I thought about it the more it sounded like a great idea. So I told Kim to make the arrangements. On a Sunday I would travel to Yokota Air Base, then take a bus to the Sano Hotel in Tokyo, which was run by the US Government, and then go by train to Osaka on Wednesday.

When I enquired about train schedules to Osaka at the hotel, the Japanese tour agent said, "You no have reservations?"

"No, I didn't think I would need them," I replied.

"Problem!" she said. "You need reservation!"

I hadn't thought about that! In my naïveté I believed bullet trains ran every half hour. So, I decided to get to the train station early.

I arrived at the station about 7:00 a.m. The station was jammed with commuters and travelers. This, too, I had not anticipated! I went to several ticket stations only to be turned down.

A one-legged man had observed me pleading with the ticket agent. He was supported by a homemade crutch. He tapped me on the shoulder and said "You go Osaka?" Since he wasn't very well dressed I took him for a con man. "You go Osaka?" he asked again. I told him I could not get on the train without a reservation.

He held out his hand and said, "I get you ticket!" I looked at my watch – about 7:40 a.m. I was desperate, so I gave him my yen, which I had been told was the cost of a round trip.

"You come!" he ordered and disappeared into the crowd.

"So that's his game!" I muttered to myself. "Even with one leg he could maneuver through the crowd and there goes my money!"

Since I was taller than most of the Japanese, over their heads I saw a crutch waving in the air. It was him.

He had worked his way down to the platform where sat the most beautiful passenger train I ever saw. It was called "The Blue Bird Special" and ran non-stop to Osaka.

Despite his handicap, he made very good time and took me to the end of the train. At the very end he opened a compartment door which was surrounded by dials and has a single seat. I started to get in when I realized this was for someone connected with the train. "I can't sit there!" I yelled out.

"You sit, train go and man come here from front of train. He no have seat. He no stop train, you sit."

"No, I won't, but thanks anyway for your help." He wasn't through yet. Standing at every entrance to each passenger car was a conductor dressed in a black uniform. All were standing at attention.

My helper started at the end of the train and stopped at each conductor pleading with him to get me aboard.

His pleas were met with utter distain, until he faces the man in the white uniform. "The train master!" The train master turned to me and beckoned me to come before him. I put the saddest look on my face that I could.

He looked me up and down (I was in uniform) snaps his fingers and one of the conductors comes running to him.

They converse in Japanese, but I could tell by their facial expressions they were talking about me. The conductor motions for me to follow him. I reached in my wallet and grabbed some yen and thrust it into my helper's hands.

A man was seated very comfortably in a seat with a table between the seats. He had his shoes off with his feet under his body like a yoga practitioner. Also, he was reading a paper.

The conductor says something to him and angrily he put on his shoes and stamped down the aisle. My other seatmates thought I must be someone of great importance. They even shared their lunches with me!

What an experience riding the Blue Bird! We must have been going 80 to 90 miles an hour, but we moved very smoothly. Osaka is far south of Tokyo and by express train it took eight hours.

The train entered the Osaka terminal at four in the afternoon, which is to say the train was right on schedule. I looked in vain for Mr. Kim. Since his future son-in-law told Kim I would be wearing a uniform, I thought at least it would be easier for him to recognize me.

I was kind of surprised not to see many US Servicemen in the terminal; as a matter of fact, I don't recall seeing any at all.

After about a half hour had lapsed, I began to be concerned. I did have his name, address and telephone number, so I figured I'd better call him.

I don't know if they still do it now, but often Japanese students would stop an American stranger and usually the conversation would start something like this: "Hey-ro (Hello). Do you spake Engrish?" Well, right about then, a young lad came up behind me and said, "Hey-ro." Before he cold say anymore I turned and said, "Yes!" I completely bewildered him!

I showed him the name of my missing host and his phone number written in Japanese. The boy looked to be about 14 or 15 years old. He kept nodding his head in the affirmative when I asked him to call the number and tell him Captain Martin was here! To do this, I spoke slowly and used a lot of body and sign language.

I thrust into his hand several coins in yen. He took off like a shot.

I waited… and waited… and waited for the longest time. I was beginning to think he had run off with my money.

Then I hear this excited "Hey-ro!" He had come back! I asked if he had talked to Mr. Kim. "No," he replied. "Who did you talk to?" I asked. He shrugged his shoulders. I realized that this was going to be a big problem.

"He no home!" He smiled when he said this. I thrust some more money in his hand. Using sign language and charade motions, I kept repeating "Where he go?" And off he went again.

And once again I was pacing the floor. It was getting dark and I was running out of coins. But he returned with a great big smile on his face. Laughing, he said, "He go Tokyo to see you!"

There I was in a city of two million people with a limited amount of Japanese currency. I did, however, have a return ticket – only it was for two days later!

After thanking and tipping the kid, I raced for a ticket counter. Struggling with words, I was finally able to exchange my ticket for the following day.

Near the train station was a large hotel and, thank goodness, the desk clerk spoke good English. I showed him how much yen I had left and asked if that would get me a room for the night. He discussed the mater with a higher up. It was quite evident that I didn't have enough! But good luck prevailed and I was given a small room with a bath. You can't believe how happy I was!

Since it was only about eight in the evening, I decided to venture out. Very few signs were in English. That was to be expected, I guess. Even so, I did not want to go too far.

There it was – a large billboard about 10 by 20 feet with the name VALERIE PRICE in big bold lettering. In smaller English words it read "O.B. THEATER." The rest was in Japanese.

I've got to back up here and give you some background. Before my club burned down, I had received a call from the civilian Officers' Club manager in Osan. He explained that Valerie Price was an exotic dancer who had recently appeared at Walkerhill in Seoul. They had paid her in Korean won, which was fluctuating in value. She wanted to be paid cash in US dollars and she wanted to get the hell out of Korea. Would I be interested in her entertaining the members of the Officers' Club for only $100 cash? He said he had contacted the club custodian for the NCO Club and he had gladly accepted the offer. It was up to him and me to arrange for a performance since she was going to be here for only one night.

The NCO custodian selected 7:00 p.m., which left me with a 9:00 p.m. performance. Since Col. Thompson and I were not seeing eye-to-eye on a lot of things, I thought it best to talk to him before I confirmed her appearance.

"Did you say an exotic dancer?" the commander bellowed. "No way!" I proceeded to tell him she could do exotic dances, but she was an accomplished performer and could sing, dance – and *not* take her clothes off.

The colonel finally calmed down and agreed to the performance only if she did not take a stitch off. It would be my ass if she did.

With that decided, I called the club manager in Osan and confirmed her appearance and told him that she was not to perform a striptease. He thought that strange, but would relay my edict.

Miss Price arrived at the front gate. She was accompanied by her bodyguard (she said) and her assistant, a German named Hans. He was a big strapping guy and I helped him unload all her wardrobe and records. One of her requirements was that we have a sound system. We did.

After getting them all settled in the VIP quarters, she asked if I could show her around the base. Sure I could! (I had already confiscated a pickup truck from the motor pool.)

Kunsan was not a pretty place, even though it was on the Yellow Sea. When the tide was out, all you could see were black mud flats. You couldn't even see the ocean. At high tide at night, though, the ocean waves lapped the shore.

Valerie Price was very beautiful, very witty and very English! All this with a figure that filled out her pantsuit very well. I took Hans and her to both clubs and she found everything to her satisfaction. We had an early dinner at the Officers' Club. If I remember accurately, she ate very little, whereas Hans devoured a big steak in minutes.

After the NCO club show, I picked her, Hans and her equipment up and prepared for the last performance.

What a show! She was a fabulous dancer and singer. Also, she was well aware of what servicemen wanted to see and hear. It was $100 well spent!

After her performance, she said she was starving. The club was still open so it was no trouble feeding her.

The next morning I drove her and Hans to Kunsan City where they took the ferry to Edi then caught the train to Seoul. From Seoul they were headed to Japan.

Now back to the story! Valerie Price in Osaka at the O.B. Theater. Now to find the O.B. Theater. After stopping several school boys and asking for directions, I finally found my way to the theater.

It was a Japanese burlesque house. Since I had no yen, I couldn't buy a ticket. I found the entrance for the entertainers. I was denied entrance by a big fellow who was probably a sumo wrestler. I wrote a quick note to Valerie with her name in large letters on the outside. He nodded his head and disappeared through the door.

About five minutes went by when the door opened and out steps Hans! "Joe!" he said. "Vat are you do-ink here?" He grabbed me by the elbow and escorted me to Valerie's dressing room. She jumped up and ran to me, threw her arms around me and, like Hans, asked "What the hell are you doing here?"

I explained my predicament. She said, "No problem. Come out and see my show!" I might add it was not like the show she put on at Kunsan!

She had one more performance after that. After dressing in casual street clothes, she announced she was starving. We went to an international restaurant – that is, the entertainers who were performing in Osaka gathered there to eat and relax. What a mixture of people! And every one of them knew Valerie!

It was the wee hours of the morning when they paid a taxi for me to go back to the hotel. I didn't get much sleep, but I didn't care. I could do that on the train.

Years later, I read about Valerie entertaining our troops in Vietnam, still at it. What a gal!

Something was Lost in Translation

Col. Thompson, the Base Commander, was invited to be one of the speakers at the ceremonies commemorating the 50th anniversary of the opening of Kunsan Harbor. I got a call from the Mayor's committeemen that they had not heard whether or not Col. Thompson would be there. So I went over to his office.

When I mentioned it to him his response was, "No, I'm not going!" I tried to express how important it was to have representation there. I had been told that Park Chung Hee, the President of Korea, the Korean Commander of the Army, Navy, and Air Force, the Governor of the Province and, naturally, the Mayor of Kunsan City would be attending along with other dignitaries.

Again, he said, "No!" emphatically.

"How about Col. Bussells?" (our Vice Commander).

"No!"

"What about Col. Blankenship (our Operations Officer)?"

"No!"

"Then who will represent the base?" I asked.

"You! If you think it's so damn important, then *you* go!"

"But, sir, I'm just a captain!" I protested.

"You heard me!" and he dismissed me with a wave of his hand

The event was about a month off so I had plenty of time to prepare my remarks. Major Kim Hung Do was a ROKAF[*] helicopter pilot with whom I had become friends. An idea popped into my head: I'll ask him to be my interpreter!

Many times he and I tried to get together to go over what I would say, but inevitably something would come up and we would have to cancel our appointment. The day of the event quickly came upon us – and I wasn't ready!

On the bumpy ride in his jeep to Kunsan City, he and I attempted to talk to no avail. We arrived at the stadium and I marveled at how big it was! It had been built as their national athletics showplace. I don't know how many people it held, but when I looked around that vast stadium all I could see was a sea of people. On the playing field, dancers in colorful costumes were really putting on a show! My thoughts immediately turned to the sights and sounds of the Olympics!

---

[*] Republic of Korea Air Force

Although President Park wasn't there, his Vice President was. So were the military brass from all the services, and many dignitaries, most of whom I didn't recognize. I sure felt insignificant!

The speeches began, and then it was my turn. With Kim beside me, I felt a little more confident. So I began with a Korean language greeting, "An nyong hashim nikka." Then I said "On behalf of the President, John F. Kennedy, our Commander and Chief, General Lemnitzer, Chief of Staff of our armed forces, General White, Chief of Staff of the United States Air force…" Kim was translating right along. "…General O'Donnell, Commander of the Air Forces in the Pacific, General Burns, Commander of the 5th Air Force, General Hutchinson, Commander of the 310th Air Division…" [and finally!] "…Colonel Thompson, Commander of Kunsan Air Base. I bring you greetings!"

I paused while Kim caught up. I was thinking – I've got to say something profound! Something they could take home with them – something to ponder!

"When you open harbors, you open men's minds!" I pontifically began. Kim started to talk then he lightly punched me in the side and said, "What did you say?" Covering my mouth and in a low whisper I said, "You know when you open harbors, ships from all nations come in."

Once again he starts talking and once again taps me and says, "Say it again." I was getting a little irritated by this time and said in a "loud" whisper, "You can learn a lot from people of all nationalities!" Immediately Kim began to talk with no pauses. I was ready to continue my profound remark, but he kept talking for maybe two minutes without letting me interject any words of wisdom.

Then he elbowed me in the side and said, "We sit down!" I sat to thunderous applause! They loved my speech!

I leaned over and asked, "What did you say?"

"I told them that you were happy as hell to be here!"

So much for meaningful speeches!

Dr. Paul Crane and Little Miss Nobody

Of all the events in which I have participated in my life, there is none that gives me greater pleasure than the one I'll share in this story.

Dr. Paul Crane and his wife Sophie visited Kunsan as the guests of my roommate, David Williams, and me. Dr. Crane was the son of missionaries and had grown up in Korea, then returned to the states for college and medical school, then came back to Korea where he and Sophie worked as medical missionaries.

On this particular visit, Dr. Crane seemed particularly despondent and, in that quiet voice of his, told us about a little girl about nine years old who had a heart problem. The way he described it, this blood vessel should have been the diameter of about a nickel, but hers was barely open. His prognosis was that if she didn't have an operation soon she would die. If only he had a heart-lung machine, he could probably save her life. There was no such machine in either Korea or Japan. If he could get her to the States, his friend, Dr. Denton Cooley, said he would take care of her at no cost, including hospital expenses! How could we get her to Houston, Texas where Dr. Cooley practiced?

I felt that Dr. Crane, although he didn't say it, was really hinting to see if the United States Air Force could do it as a mercy flight. Once a month, a med evacuation airplane passed thru Kunsan to pick up any service people who had been injured and fly them to Japan for further treatment. Taking the hint, I told Dr. Crane I would be glad to explore the possibilities.

The next day (a Monday) I went to see the Base Commander, Col. Glenn Thompson, and his response was as I expected: "Hell, no! Those flights are for American servicemen, their dependants and civilian employees. You should know that!"

Col. Thompson didn't own the Air Force, so I looked for other support. Col. Dean Hess was the 5th Air Force Information Officer at our headquarters in Japan. He was a very Christian person. He was also the author of the well-known book, *Battle Hymn*. Col. Hess was receptive to the idea and told me to proceed. He emphasized that if the Air Force was to do this mission, he would need more information and documentation.

Happily, I called Dr. Crane and went over the talk I had with Col. Hess and the requirements needed to get on with it. Dr. Crane said if I could come down to the Missionary Hospital the following morning he would take me to see the young girl. I really didn't know what to expect.

The next morning, I arrived in Chong Ju where the hospital was located. Then Dr. Crane loaded his medical bag into his Land Rover along with some rice and other vegetables and off we went. I can't even remember the direction we went, but after an hour of driving he cut off the two-lane highway we were on and started up a dirt road. A large mountain loomed up in front of us. Pretty soon the dirt road disappeared and we started traveling over very rough terrain. He put the Land Rover in four-wheel drive and began the climb up the mountain. The mountain was barren of trees – only young saplings and shrubs were growing. As I mentioned in an earlier story, during their occupancy, the Japanese had literally raped Korea of all vegetation for their own use.

The ascent was slow, and we were being jarred about because there was no discernable road, although I could somewhat make out what appeared to be cart tracks. Then Dr. Crane said, "You know, Joe, the villagers told me I was the first person ever to drive a vehicle to visit their area! Now you'll be the second!"

"Just great!" I thought. Here we were being pioneers to go find a young girl, get her to the States, have this awesome operation and get her back home to this God-forsaken spot in Korea.

"You know, Joe, the village is not on any map. The natives call it Mon-Sur-Ree, which means "Hawk's Nest.""

Now I'm from the hills of Virginia and I know a little about mountaineers, or hillbillies, if you prefer, who exist with no running water or indoor toilets and eke out a living in shacks on a small patch of ground. My first sight of Mon-Sur-Ree was not quite the same. True, they had no running water, no sewer system, and their hatched roofed houses were not the same style as log or wood cabins, but at least a village in the area where I grew up had streets, often times paved.

The whole village turned out to greet us. I would estimate about 300 men, women and children all came out. We were looking around, trying to spot the young girl, and started walking towards what appeared to be a wooden structure that was used to cook food, which had a rickety porch. A tiny young girl sat there on her haunches with her face buried on her knees.

Dr. Crane called softly to her. He was fluent in Korean having been raised there by missionary parents. Even though he called her name several times, she would not look up. Members of her family tried to get her to at least look up.

Eventually she did. Her face showed that she was absolutely terrified of these two strangers who were paying so much attention to her. Finally, she came to her feet wearing a native dress called a chima, which was dirty and had holes in it. She never spoke, she would only nod her head as she kept her gaze fixed straight at the ground.

When she finally stood up, I could instantly tell she was very small and thin for her age. Dr. Crane had a long conversation with her father while the rest of her family and the villagers looked on. Dr. Crane told me that they could not begin to comprehend what we had in store for her. After distributing the food and some gifts for the children, we left around two in the afternoon.

I too, had a problem comprehending what was going to happen to this little girl, Little Miss Nobody. What was the value to the US Air Force, from a public relations point of view, of going to all the trouble to fly her to the States and back? I must say that it was a hell of a task for so little payback. Is her life worth that much?

Things started to happen. One of the concerns was who would accompany her. She spoke no English and we would be lucky if she spoke at all, even in Korean. The answer came when Dr. Crane called me with the news that her uncle would go with her. Her uncle was about 17 years old from a small city in the foothills. He spoke a little English, and Dr. Crane thought, with the help of a Korean/English translation book, he could get by.

Even though he was excited to go, he was apprehensive about the trip. He had never been on an airplane and didn't have any money. Where would he stay during her recovery? All these problems raced through his mind.

His problems were easier to deal with than ours. Up the command line some 5th AF staffers started questioning the whole thing. "Tell me again who she is? Is she a war orphan? Who's going to pay for all this? Are we going to have to bring her back?" But my biggest problem was my neck – which was on the chopping block.

I had briefed Col. Hess as to her environment and living conditions after our visit to the village. When he reviewed the situation, he announced that he was having a tough time convincing his higher ups that Air Force participation was essential. Couldn't the villagers raise the money to fly her and a chaperone to the States? And Col. Thompson wasn't too happy about it at all; he figured it was just another one of my stunts.

After days of waiting, approval was given by someone in PACAF[*] Command. That someone was Four Star General "Rosie" O'Donnell. The preparations began in earnest.

The med evac plane was to arrive Wednesday morning. Dr. Crane would bring the girl and her uncle to the missionary compound to stay overnight and then bring them to Kunsan early the next morning. When they arrived at the base, the girl was wearing a very plain dress with little flowers on it. Her head was still bowed. Her uncle looked terrified at the prospect of going to the land of the big BX, as the local Koreans called it. The modified C-131 landed on time and the nurse attendants warmly greeted the twosome. The plane's door closed and off they went.

Dr. Crane and his wife and a few of the missionaries stayed on for lunch. He was elated. He admitted he had had his doubts when he learned of the response I received from my superiors after our visit to the village.

Dr. Crane heard from Dr. Cooley soon after that. The operation was successful and the girl was making an excellent recovery. Dr. Cooley also said she was eating like a horse, even though the American food was not to her liking.

.[*] Pacific Air Force

I wish I could remember how long we waited, but after a time, the day for her return finally arrived. Dr. Crane, his wife, and a whole entourage of people, his staff, villagers, and others were there waiting. It was quite a reception!

The cabin door of the Air America C-131 opened, the gangway descended and there stood a Korean girl in a frilly white dress waving feverishly to the awaiting crowd. Behind her was her uncle wearing a very large cowboy hat that he doffed and waved at the assembly. I almost didn't recognize her. She had gained so much weight and was so exuberant. Not the rail thin, overly shy little girl that I remembered. Even Col. Thompson was there grinning at the show.

The leading newspaper in Seoul, *Ilebon*, headlined the occasion. In an editorial they pondered why a great country like the United States of America would take a little girl – entirely unknown except to her family and villagers – fly her across a vast ocean to a Texas city where a world-renowned heart specialist would perform a life-saving and very expensive operation, keep her in a hospital free of charge, and then return her to her remote village in the mountain and not require her to make speeches, raise monies for others or do anything like that. When a person of great renown lay ill, the whole country comes to his bedside and much money is sent in to cure him. We pray as a nation for his recovery. But a little girl who is unknown and could never afford the cure is given this gift. Could it be that this is what the Americans call *democracy* – that we regard the value of an individual no matter how unimportant he or she may be?

Yes, folks, that is a great explanation for the word democracy!

A miracle had happened! I get all teary eyed when I call up the story from my memory. To this day, I cannot forget her beautiful, happy face on that bright sunny day – as bright as the flowers she held in her hands.

My Farewell Party

Part of my job of being an Information Officer was being the Community Relations Officer. Basically, it was my job to get along with the Mayor of Kunsan City and his staff. On a higher level, the Governor of the province was in my bailiwick. Also, the base and its organizations supported five orphanages and I was Chairman of the committee responsible for monitoring our support. Add to that our work with the missionaries at the Chong Ju Presbyterian Hospital. I was also working with the United States Information Agency, which sent propaganda to schools and universities in Korea about democracy. Their representative to Kunsan and other bases was Edgar Noel who became a good friend.

I was frequently invited to parties given by the mayor, newspaper editors, radio stations, owners and others. At these functions, I experienced many unusual (to me) Asian dishes. More often than not, these all-male parties were served by Kae Sang girls.

You've no doubt heard of the Japanese Geisha girls – who were very well trained in dance, singing and conversation and were very cultured in the history and traditions of their country. In other words, they were refined ladies. The Kae Sang girls were not as refined, but were several steps above a serving maid. At these parties, the girls would reach with their chopsticks into a pot on a turntable, pull something out which goes directly to our open mouths and, with what little English they knew, would say something like "Numba One Korean food!"

I must say I developed the world's best ability to swallow! Once it was in my mouth, I would try to chew it. If it tasted good I went on chewing. If it didn't after one chomp, I would see if I could swallow it… and pray that it would stay down!

That was part of my reason to have a farewell party. The other reason was to invite people whom I really liked and to whom I wanted to say thank you.

To this end, I ordered pickled pigs feet, jalapeño peppers, beef jerky and peanut butter! The Koreans love peanuts, but not once did I see them eating peanut butter. Naturally, I had other food like steak, which I knew they would enjoy.

For a beverage, I had Coca-Cola. But for hard liquor, I ordered bottles of Lemon Hart rum, which is the best rum in the world as far as I was concerned. I understand it was distilled someplace in the British Guianas. The kick was it had an alcohol content somewhere between 150 and 160 proof!

To help serve my guests, I hired three Kae Sang girls. My two roommates, Captain David Williams and Army First Lieutenant, Reed Bennett, helped me plan the event.

We were all seated on pillows around a square. The Kae Sangs served our food in courses on plates or in bowls. I would stand up, take a jalapeño pepper, hold my head back, open my mouth and drop the whole pepper in my mouth. Once the pepper was in my mouth, without making a face, I would exclaim, "Number one American food!" My Korean guests attempted to emulate me. You've heard of the inscrutable Oriental? Don't you believe it! They suffer pain like you and me... and they showed it!

Frantically, they reached for their glass of Coke (which was laced with rum), hoping to deaden the burning sensation.

Then I would get a spoonful of peanut butter and eat it and again "Number one American food!" Have you ever seen a baby eating its first bite of peanut butter? You remember how it looked as it stuck to the roof of its mouth? Well, the same with my guests. Once again, they grabbed for the rum and Coke to get it down.

The party started around six and ended about midnight. Not one of my Korean guests – including the Kae Sang girls – left under his or her own power. At one point, the mayor got up to make a toast. He raised his glass and that was as far as he got. He literally wilted and passed out on the floor.

The Governor of the province was no better. He sat there cross-legged like a Buddha with his hands over his belly. He had a placid smile on his face. I thought he was asleep – he was. His driver tried to help him to his feet but he was completely blotto!

There were no sober guests left. Everyone had to be helped to their cars. Thank goodness there were several sober drivers and enough cars to get everyone home.

Later, my replacement wrote to me at my new base and said they were still talking about "that party!"

The Koreans have a phrase: "Set yourself free." If one of the men drinks too much, he is said to have "set himself free" and others will take care of him. I was glad to have been able to bring a little American-made freedom to Korea during my stay!

Homestead

Turns out, Dad's return from Korea didn't sit particularly well with one particular lady in his life – his baby daughter, Melissa Constance Martin. She, after all, had not one but three women – her mother, grandmother and great-grandmother – living with her and taking care of her while Dad was away. All that around-the-clock pampering suited her just fine.

Then, in January of 1964, this strange man *suddenly comes into their lives, kidnaps them, and takes them to Homestead AFB, Florida. Not only does Melissa lose two out of her three handmaidens, but this stranger expects her number-one servant – her Mother – to pay attention to* him *and take care of* his *needs. (It's not just that he was home again. In his time in Korea, Dad had grown accustomed to having his every domestic whim satisfied by his "me washee and shinee shoes" mamasan. Mom is still trying to help Dad unlearn his learned helpless from those days long ago.) Worse yet, I was born nine months to the day after Dad's return stateside. It's enough to make a young toddler run away, which Missy attempted with some regularity.*

But this book isn't about the escapades of the Martin progeny; it is about the progenitor. We now find our hero back in the US, as our hero finds himself *getting into mischief once again…*

Neil Davis and the Dirty Movie

I believe it was in the late spring of 1963 that I briefly deployed along with a squadron of F100s and support groups bound for McClelland AFB near Sacramento, California. The exercise was "Desert Strike" and the purpose was to practice close air support with the Army.

One weekend, I left by bus to San Francisco and on to Sausalito, the Greenwich Village of San Francisco, just across the Golden Gate Bridge. It was a quaint area with great bayside restaurants, interesting shops, and was a haven for the hippies, writers and artists.

My friend Neil Davis owned a well-known bar named, well, it was the "No Name Bar." All top-drawer liquor, it catered to the working artists and writers. The bartenders all wore ties and the good-looking waitresses wore mini-skirts. What I want to tell you about is my meeting with Neil.

By the middle of a pleasantly warm sunny Saturday afternoon, I went into the bar where Neil was waiting for me in a quiet area. He ordered drinks, wine for him and bourbon for me. While we were reminiscing about days gone by, I hear footsteps. Turning around I see this gorgeous creature with a shapely body who displayed her contours in this very tight dress.

Hi, Neil!" she said in a very soothing voice. "When do we start shooting?" I know I must have drooled out of the corner of my mouth because my head was cocked to the side.

"Oh," he replied nonchalantly, "in a couple of more weeks. We've had some technical problems." "I'll call you when we get them ironed out."

"Please do," she cooed.

I watched her sashay out of the bar. It took me a while to regain my composure. "Who's *that*!" I said showing no restraint.

"She's my star," answering me as if he really didn't care.

"Your *star*?" I practically yelled out, "What *kind* of star?"

"My movie star," he answered.

"Your *movie* star?" I scarcely could believe what he told me.

"We're making a movie."

"A movie? What *kind* of movie?"

Instead of answering me directly he asked me a question. "Did you ever see *The Immoral Mr. Teas*?"

It didn't take me too long to answer, "No, but I did see the pictures in *Playboy*!"

"Well, you know when Mr. Teas put on those, let's say, magic glasses, the women's clothing came off?"

"Yeah, I do."

"This is a little different. Instead of glasses, I'm using one of the old stereopticon viewers, you remember the kind that Grandpa had. Instead of scenery, people, buildings, whatever, the photos were of women and when seen through the viewer their clothes are off."

"They're naked?" I asked.

"Yeah, that's right and the lady you met is my "star," but I have others," he explained.

"You mean you can find women willing to pose naked? What does it cost to make a film like this?"

"Mr. Teas cost about $27,000 to film – and that included all the lighting, sound people and directors. Now for the good part – it grossed over $1.3 million!"

"Are you doing the directing?" I asked.

"Oh no," he replied. "I'm merely financing the movie. I reckon by the cost estimates I've been given, the movie will cost about $34,000. I've even found a company to distribute it."

"Wow!" I could hardly contain myself.

Then he asks, "Are you interested in being one of the investors?"

What an opportunity, I thought. "Sure!" I said very confidently.

"Ok, I'll send you a prospectus".

"No need for that," I replied. "I'll take your word for it."

"How much are you wanting to invest?"

Sonia and I had $2,000 and some odd change in our savings account. That was our total life savings – no stocks, no bonds – that was it! "I'll go in for $2,000," trying to be as casual as I could about it.

"All right," said Neil. "But, I still want you to have a prospectus because there's a risk that we might lose money."

"I'll send you the money just as soon as I get home!" Which I did.

Not too long after that Sonia said, "I don't know what to believe. I went to the bank today to draw out some money from our savings account and they said there was only a few dollars in there!"

"Oh, Sonia, I meant to tell you – uh, it was gonna be a surprise!" I said. "Neil Davis is producing a movie. When I was out there a couple of weeks ago he told me about it."

"What kind of film is it?" she asked.

"It's kind of a soft porn, I think they call it. It should be a real money maker and I invested our $2,000 in it."

"You *what*?" Sonia exploded. "You invested our money in one of those dirty movies?"

"Well, hon, let me tell you about it," I pleaded.

"You're not telling me anything. You are going to get our money back! That's final!"

I quickly wrote Neil a letter telling him of my predicament. In no time, he airmailed my $2,000 back. Attached to a piece of cardboard was two pennies.

Neil never did make that movie. Good thing I got my money back – with interest!

Meeting Bob Hope

In 1964, when I was stationed at Homestead AFB, Florida as a Public Information Officer, the Pentagon advised me by TWX (a teletype message) that Bob Hope was gathering several entertainers to go to Santo Domingo to entertain the troops.

Our armed forces were in Santo Domingo to separate two warring factions. In the TWX, headquarters asked if I could find a suitably large rehearsal hall at or near the Miami Airport. I called Miami International Airport and found they did in fact have a theater – with a stage and all. I forwarded this information.

Everything began to fall into place. My job was to meet Bob Hope when he arrived by private plane and escort him to the rehearsal hall. My boss, Colonel James Jabara, the Wing Commander, was requested to be there with me to greet Mr. Hope. (Colonel Jabara was the first MIG Ace of the Korean War. Shot down five of them!)

Hope's plane arrived on schedule and Colonel Jabara and I were there to greet him. When he got off the plane, I introduced Colonel Jabara. Hope seemed genuinely pleased to meet the famous ace. After the brief formalities, he turned to me and asked, "Are you going to take me to the rehearsal hall?" I said yes. He excused himself from Colonel Jabara, took me aside, and instructed me to take the most direct route to the hall "and *do not stop* for any reason *no matter what I say to you.*"

"Yes, sir, Mr. Hope."

Miami's airport terminal is quite large. His plane had landed at one end and the hall was at the other end on the second floor. So we had a lot of ground to cover.

We started out. He had a golf club in his hand – an iron. I thought I was walking at a pretty good pace, but before we reached the main terminal I heard him say, "Faster!"

We were walking at a very rapid pace when we entered the main terminal. I could see people doing the double take – that's Bob Hope! – and gravitate towards him.

"Slow down, Captain!" he would yell. "I want to meet these folks!" Remembering my strict orders, I pressed on. He used the golf club very effectively. When people came closer he would take the club at arm's length, extend the club and aim it at them. This way they would pause giving him enough time to get away. "Sorry, folks," he'd say as he tried to catch up yelling, "Slow down, Captain!"

The technique was very effective – we made it to the rehearsal hall in no time!

Rehearsing for the Tour

Bob Hope's entourage included comedian Jerry Colona, the big-eyed vaudevillian, the actress Tuesday Weld, and the beautiful singer-dancer Joey

Heatherton. The Les Brown Band and a chorus line of dancers, singers and other acts supported the headliners.

I was fortunate to be able to sit in the back of the rehearsal hall and watch the proceedings. Bob Hope was in complete control. No doubt about it. There were people assisting him, but he had the final word.

Jerry Colona was getting old. He and Bob Hope had been together in their vaudevillian days and had become very good friends. Jerry's mental ability was not nearly as quick as Bob Hope's. Practicing their routine, Jerry repeatedly missed several cues or lines. Bob would patiently explain to Jerry the skit outline and give him leads. Unfortunately, Jerry still screwed up. Still Bob did not berate him. He merely changed the skit to make it simpler.

The other entertainers did not fare as well. When Joey Heatherton muffed a line or missed a dance step with him, Hope exploded! "You dizzy blonde, can't you get that straight? You're supposed to be a professional!" he would bellow.

The following morning after one day of rehearsals in Miami, an Air Force C-130 cargo plane picked up the troupe and flew them to Santo Domingo. I heard they put on a terrific show!

How to Talk to Fighter Pilots

I'll always be indebted to the late Col. James Jabara, the Korean MIG ace and my Commander at the 31st Tactical Fighter Wing at Homestead AFB, Florida.

My previous assignments had been at Systems Command where I met pilots – not all of them fighter pilots, which are a distinct breed! And during my tour of duty in Korea I met many bomber pilots who were also easy to talk to.

As an information officer with the 31st, I would visit the operations offices of the four squadrons of F-100s, hoping to get a story or an idea for a story. Most of the time all I got was a cold shoulder. It was quite evident that I was a "slick wing" – or non-rated – and, therefore, the pilots didn't seem to care one way or the other about my problems.

I had had enough! I really hated to admit it to him, but I went to see Col. Jabara to ask for his advice and help. Col. Jabara was a very self-effacing person, short and wiry, not the image of a "real" fighter ace. After listening to my plight he said he had a story that might help me. Then he began.

"I joined the Army Air Corps in WWII. It seemed all my life I wanted to be a fighter pilot. Most of my training in primary and basic flying training took place in Florida. After completing the training, I found out they said I graduated first in my class and would have my choice of assignments.

"My choice was to take an assignment with the newly formed British Royal Air Force squadron flying Spitfires. Do you remember the Spitfire?" he asked.

"I sure do! The battle of Britain was won in the skies! And the Spitfires played a large part in that victory!"

Col. Jabara agreed and went on with his story. "I mentioned that this squadron of 18 Spitfires was newly formed and most of us had never been in an air battle. It was a small base, but we did have decent quarters even if they were Quonset huts. We had a dining hall, recreation room and even an Officers' Club.

"Most days four or five of us would take off and fly over our sector, looking for enemy planes. Usually, we were up 20, maybe 30, minutes because our planes were not equipped with auxiliary fuel tanks and we'd come home.

"When we entered the club, a crusty old US Army major, our tactical lesson officer, would usually be sitting at the bar. The first thing he would do is yell at me 'Hey, Jabara, come over here!'

"You've got to remember I was a 2nd lieutenant and he was a major. A big difference! He'd say, 'Jabara, what did you flyboys do today? Did you get any enemy?' I would respond 'No, sir, we flew over sector [something or other], but didn't engage any enemy aircraft.' He would counter with, 'How long were you up today, Jabara? 10 minutes? 20 minutes?' 'Sir, we were up 23 minutes today.' I would factually answer his question.

"'Let's see now Jabara, you got up this morning, had a real nice breakfast meal in the dining hall, flew, how long did you say you were up today?' 'Twenty-three minutes, sir!' 'Yeah, and you land and come over to the Officers' Club to have a drink of scotch, go back to your quarters and go to bed between two clean sheets... and for all that you get "flying pay"?

"'Let me ask you, Jabara – have you ever eaten a C-Ration?' 'No, sir.' 'Have you ever slept in a muddy fox hole?' 'No, sir.' 'Have you ever had real bullets fired at you or been shelled?' 'No, sir.' He would conclude his remarks with 'You get flying pay!' and shake his head. It got so I dreaded walking into the Officers' Club for fear of seeing him. But I toughed it out and took his guff.

"One day, me and several of our planes went up. The Luftwaffe came out of nowhere! The air battle was over in ten minutes. But in that short time we lost two planes along with their pilots and several other planes were damaged. We managed to limp back to base, but I was devastated! I had lost two of my friends and I was grieving.

"I wasn't even thinking of the major when I walked into the Officers' Club. But then I heard his voice and my grieving turned into anger. I automatically clenched my fists. That son of a bitch! If he says one word I'll hit him. I don't care if they court marshal me. There was fire in my eyes when I went over to him.

"Surprisingly, he put his hand over my shoulder and in a soft voice said, 'I heard what happened today and I just want you to know how sorry I am!'

"I didn't know what to say. He went on 'I know I've been giving you a hard time about your extra flying pay, but I want you to know you deserve every penny of it! You gotta remember – the Luftwaffe has been doing this for years. They have all the experience and tactics. So eventually it had to happen. If it was left up to me, I would increase your flying pay.'

'Thank you, sir;' I said, still in shock over what had happened, which was now compounded by his concern. As I started to break away he said, 'Jabara, what in the hell do you guys do to earn your base pay?'"

I thanked Col. Jabara profoundly. That was my entry!

I hustled over to the 307th Fighter Squadron. There at the flight operations desk sat a captain reading "Flying Magazine". I cleared my throat, which caused him to look up and I asked in a very sincere voice. "Help me, Captain, if you would. I know what you do for your flying pay, but what do you do to earn your base pay?"

We began a real conversation. Thank you, again, Col. Jabara!

Las Vegas

What a great gig – Public Information Officer for Nellis AFB in Las Vegas! I'm sure it had its headaches, but it seems like Dad spent much of his time hobnobbing with celebrities during his brief stint there from October 1965 to May 1967. Not a bad job for a pilot training washout!

The Jimmy Stewart Story

The ABC Television Network sought permission from the Department of Defense to do an hour long special about a fighter group in Vietnam. Nellis AFB, near Las Vegas, had been selected for the beginning and end of the film. Most of the other film footage had been taken in Vietnam.

The Pentagon asked me to prepare a 30-second intro and a 45-second conclusion for the film. Jimmy Stewart had agreed to do the narrative. I was to write the script for Mr. Stewart and then submit it to the Pentagon to be cleared and edited as needed.

I was doubly excited since the Air Force wing that was being featured was the 31st Tactical Fighter Wing stationed at Ben Hoa, Vietnam. I had been the Public Information Officer for the 31st when I was stationed at Homestead AFB, Florida. The 31st flew the F-100 Saberjet. The reason Nellis was selected was that it was the home of the Tactical Fighter Weapons Center, which had F-100s and Jimmy Stewart was asked because he was a retired Brigadier General.

I eagerly accepted the task (I really had no choice) and prepared several intros and exit scripts for the Pentagon to review. They returned the scripts to me with minor modifications.

The date was set for Jimmy Stewart's arrival. An F-100 had been parked where the ABC film crew thought best for the scene angle.

Mr. Stewart arrived at McCarren Airport in Las Vegas on the early flight from Las Angeles. I was there in a staff car to meet him.

It was going to be a hot, dry day. Mr. Stewart had on a dark brown suit, white shirt, dark tie and wore a "man's" hat. I don't know why, but I kinda expected him to show up in his general's uniform.

From the airport, I drove directly to the base so he could meet the Center Commander, Base Commander, and other staff members. After exchanging niceties, we proceeded to the flight line. I think it was about 9:30 a.m.

The F-100 sat glistening in the bright sunshine. The ABC crew had just about completed their setup. When Mr. Stewart arrived, they checked to confirm their camera settings, etc. A make-up person started dabbing Mr. Stewart's face.

Ready for the rehearsal! Mr. Stewart posed in front of the fighter jet on the side of the wing tip. But he still was not satisfied. Much to the consternation of the film crew, he had lighting changed and cameral angles altered. After all, he had been in the movie business for a number of years.

The script! I kept wondering when he would get to it. During make-up he scanned the words. While the cameras rolled he rehearsed the lines. Over and over again! I think they're called "takes" where you can review the film and narration. He evidently was a quick study because he had the lines memorized in no time at all. But he still did not like the end result!

He came over to me and said in his well-known Indiana drawl, "Joe, the script is good… but it's not me. It's not the way I talk," he continued.

"Mr. Stewart, change it any way you want," I said. "Consider it an outline of what the Pentagon approved."

"How's this sound?" he asked me. He proceeded to give the script his flavoring. It was very good and he did it without changing the meaning.

Rehearsal began anew. The film crew was wilting. What they thought would be about an hour – rehearsal, shoot, put it in the can – turned out to be several hours. It was past noon with a few breaks to drink gallons of cold water and soft drinks. By about one thirty it was finally over. He still looked like it was nothing at all. My summer uniform, which was well creased when I picked him up, had sweat stains all over it.

"I've made arrangements for you to stay overnight at the Desert Inn," I said.

"Oh, no, Joe. I want to get back to Los Angeles as soon as I can."

"I've got that option covered too. You're booked on a four o'clock flight. However, the folks down at the Desert Inn are expecting you."

"Let's have lunch there then, Joe. I am mighty hungry."

We arrived at the Desert Inn about noon. Mr. Stewart said, "Let's duck into a nice, cool room and have a drink." I wholeheartedly agreed.

We found a small room where they put on cabaret style shows. It was dark and cool. A cocktail waitress came into the room. "Don't you know we're closed here?" She sounded exasperated. Then she came over closer and said, "Are you who I think you are?"

I stood up and said, "Damn, I can't go any place without getting attention!"

She came closer to me and said, "I think I've seen you in some television spots." Then she turned to Mr. Stewart. "You're Jimmy Stewart!" she exclaimed.

"Yes," he replied quietly.

In well modulated tones she said, "How are things in Los Angeles, Jimmy?" putting on her best actress voice. "I found Los Angeles to be a drag. So I came to Vegas for the excitement!"

Mr. Stewart broke in. "Can we get something cool?"

"For you, you certainly can!"

So we ordered drinks. It was getting close to three and Mr. Stewart said, "Let's grab a quick bite – I'm really hungry!"

"The Desert Inn has a nice informal dining room," I said. "Let's go there."

Upon entering the restaurant, a loud voice called out, "Jimmy!" It was Ed Sullivan and he was frantically motioning with both hands for him to come over to his table. He was hosting several people from the entertainment world, most of whom I didn't recognize.

Mr. Stewart took me by the elbow and escorted me to meet Mr. Sullivan. Graciously, Mr. Sullivan started introducing me to everyone at the table, starting with his wife, Sylvia. After the introductions, Mr. Stewart excused us by saying he had a plane to catch at four.

I know everyone in the place was staring at us. Loud whispers – "That's Jimmy Stewart!" He found us a booth in a relatively quiet area. We ordered sandwiches.

It was not too long after ordering that Jack Walsh, the executive director of the Desert Inn, and his higher ups in the casino, trooped in to see Mr. Stewart.

He made the plane in time, but just barely.

What a day! I've always enjoyed Mr. Stewart's acting ability, but I came to respect his professionalism. Even though his performance was short, he had them film that segment over and over again until they got it right – according to *his* standards, not theirs!

Sammy Davis, Jr. – The Complete Entertainer

Sammy Davis, Jr. was appearing in Las Vegas. His manager called me and said, "Sammy would like to entertain our servicemen at the base." He went on to explain that Sammy had some time off before he began his appearances at The Sands casino. He would have his band with him and his people would take care of everything. All he needed was a stage on which to perform his act.

I presented the idea to the Center Commander, who was delighted to have the famous singer, dancer, actor and comedian appear for the troops. He told me to work with the Chief of Maintenance, the famous fighter pilot, Colonel John Black – or "Black Jack" as he preferred to be called – to approve the facilities.

"Black Jack" wasn't happy about it. He wasn't happy about it because the Vietnam War was in full swing. He and his people were working overtime to keep the planes used to train pilots flying. He was behind schedule, but a general outranks a colonel, so a hanger was made ready for Sammy Davis, Jr.

The show was scheduled for late afternoon. His band, soundmen and others arrived earlier to set up and check everything out before his arrival. Just before Sammy arrived, his manager came to me and said, "Sammy and his people will need some refreshments because of the heat." I agreed and said we've arranged for ice, soft drinks, and water to be at the hanger in time for the performance. "That's fine, but Sammy has some special requirements: Two bottles of Stoli vodka, one bottle Absolut, one bottle of bourbon and set ups like quinine water, mixes, cokes and the like."

I was stunned! We had no base funds for that, so I quickly sought out General Taylor, the Center Commander, who reached in his pocket and pulled out folding money. The rest I charged at the Officers' Club – hoping to take a collection later for the rest of the money.

When the booze and set ups were delivered back stage, Mr. Davis poured himself a water glass full of bourbon and drank it down with one swig! I know my eyes popped out. He then proceeded to have another and another.

"Oh, God!" I thought. "He's gonna get sloshed and make a fool of himself… and there goes my career." I couldn't bear to watch him any longer, so I left to go backstage.

The band started an overture, dancers came out and the show began. It was the same show they were going to do at The Sands. Then the drums rolled and the bugles blew a fanfare. Here he came – and with the agility of a cat, he jumped onto the stage and went into a song. He was sensational!

The Final Mission

A few days before I was to transfer from Nellis AFB, Nevada to Wright-Patterson AFB, Ohio, I was still working as the Public Information Officer. I went into my office slightly before 7:00 a.m. and the phone was ringing. It was General Zack Taylor's secretary telling me to report to the General's office at once. "Now what have I done?" I thought to myself. Since I could not recall any discrepancy I had recently committed, I walked into his office with an open mind.

"Joe," he said. "I want you to go to the Command Post and check to see what flights we had up this morning." That was an easy task because the Command Center was in the headquarters building. After talking to the officer in charge, I found out that we had a flight of two F-105 Thunderjets on the gunnery range. With this information, I reported back to General Taylor. When I arrived back in his office, Colonel Ventura, the Staff Judge Advocate, and Captain Greenspan, the Claims Officer were there. About the same time, an airman from the base photo lab reported. General Taylor then began to explain the reason for this hurry up meeting.

"I got a call from Charles Bell from Nevada Senator Bering's Office that a flight of four jet fighters had dumped paper all over a resort area named Ash Meadows." With that news, I started to chuckle out loud.

"What's so damn funny, Joe?"

"Sir, do you know what Ash Meadows is?" I asked.

"No, I don't!" he emphatically said.

I didn't quite know how to put it, so I just laid it out. "Well, uh, sir, it's a fly-in whorehouse!"

"Captain," said the General, looking disgusted at me. "This was Charles Bell, Senator Bering's Chief Administrative Aide!"

"That figures, sir. I know Charlie."

Changing the subject, he demanded, "What did the command post say?"

"We had two F-105s up on the gunnery range east of Indian Springs." I replied.

Then the General turned to Colonel Ventura and said, "I want this investigated and you are to report back to me when you return." Turning to me he said "You get a staff car and take everyone to Ash Meadows and take plenty of pictures."

"Yes, sir," we all said in unison, saluted and left his office.

Outside Colonel Ventura asked, "Where in the hell is Ash Meadows?" I tried to explain to him that I had only heard of the place and thought it was somewhere near the California border. I had a map of Nevada in my personal car and lo and behold there was Ash Meadows, in very small print, with the silhouette of an airplane denoting a landing strip. You take the main highway from Las Vegas to Los Angeles and, about an hour away, head north on a paved two-lane highway. Ash Meadows, we guessed, was about an hour from there.

The highway was flat and straight as an arrow and you could see ahead for miles. Soon, I spotted a white car in the distance coming toward us. I remembered Charlie Bell had a white Ford Thunderbird with Senator Bering's name emblazoned on the side of it. There were no other cars on the road at that time, so I started slowing down. As the white car came nearer, I pulled off the road and got out.

The white car was traveling very fast since there were no speed limits at that time. I stood partially in the road and started waving my hands. The car slowed down, drove past me, and stopped about 50 yards past us. As it went by, I thought I saw someone in the front seat duck down.

Charlie jumped out of the car and yelled, "Joe, what the hell are you doing here?"

"You call, we haul," I said as I walked towards his car.

Charlie came running towards me. "Who's all here?" He strained to get a look.

"I've got the Staff Judge Advocate, the Claims Officer and a photographer."

"No need for that, Joe," he said taking my arm.

"Charlie, you called the General and said a flight of four aircraft dumped paper all over a resort hotel. He sent us here to investigate the incident."

Charlie looked pained. "Look, Joe," he said, sounding as reassuring as he could. "I'll call the General and get this all straightened out."

"You can do that Charlie, but we've got our orders and were going to investigate the matter."

"Damn it Joe, you know what Ash Meadows is! Those airplanes were so low they damn near took the roof off the houses. The noise jarred me out of bed. The owner wants this mess cleaned up."

"We'll see about that Charlie," I said. "By the way, who's in the front seat with you? They still have not come up for air. Was that Woody Cole?"

"Damn it, Joe," he pleaded, "keep that quiet!" Woodrow Cole was the "high" sheriff for Clark County, the seat of which is Las Vegas.

"Yes, it should not be known," I agreed.

We proceeded up the road. A sign with an arrow pointed east and simply read "Ash Meadows." At first it looked like a dilapidated ranch. The barns and other out buildings had either fallen down or looked as though they were about to. Rusty wagons and farm equipment were outside the building. The main house was a one story wooden structure, rustic in design. Small individual pieces of toilet paper like you find in latrines were all over the place. Reminded you of a "TP-ing" party, but instead of streams of toilet paper these were pieces. Inside, however, still in western style was a large dining area with red checkered tablecloths, a bar area and a small room with slot machines. A rather large, attractive redhead in her 40s gaped as we paraded into the establishment.

"There you are," she said raising her voice. "Are you here to clean up this mess?"

"No, Ma'am," I said. "We're here to investigate the low flying aircraft that dropped paper over your compound."

"Hell, I don't want an investigation! I thought Charlie told me he was going to have some of you Air Force people pick all this crap up!"

To which I replied, "The General wants us first to find out who did it. We're from Nellis and we didn't have any planes over this way.

I had a book with all types of current Air Force aircraft. I turned to the fighter section and showed a picture of an F-105. The bartender joined in the screening. "Not that," he said. I turned the page to an F-4. "Nope, not that type." On the next page, an F-100. "That's it! They're the ones!"

The nearest Air Force Base with F-100's was George AFB located at Victorville, California. I felt we had pinned down the culprits. "Do any of the fellows from George AFB ever come over here?"

"Yeah, there was a bunch of them over here last night. They were having a hell of a party. I gathered some of them were leaving for Vietnam today."

I finally asked her a direct question. "Do you have any idea, why they might want to do this?"

She became very thoughtful and after a bit came to a conclusion. "I think one of them said he got a bad lay!"

We bid our good-byes. As we were going through the entrance she called out, "Is anyone gonna clean this mess up?"

Upon our return, we briefed the General. "Not long after you left, I got a call from Charles Bell saying he acted in haste and there was no real damage to Ash Meadows. He was more concerned about the safety of the pilots who did this."

Later, I got a call from Charlie Bell. "Please keep your mouth shut, Joe!"

I think the statute of limitations on my promise to keep quiet is up by now.

Part 4
My Friend, Gary Collier

Of all the colorful characters that show up in Dad's stories, one name seems to get more than its fair share of airtime – Gary Collier. Added together, they tell a tale worthy of its own section.

The Mystery Man in the Back Booth

Aside from Paul McConnell, one of my earliest friends was Gary Collier. When I was about four or five, Gary's grandmother would often bring him into town and drop him off at my house.

Gary's mother was a 6th-grade teacher. His father had also been a teacher when they lived in Georgia. One day, while his father was writing something on the blackboard, a student crept up, pulled a knife and, before any of the kids could alert him, stabbed him in the back. He soon died from his wound. After that, Mrs. Collier brought Gary and his younger brother Eugene to live with her mother in the country just outside Big Stone.

Gary walked to the beat of a different drummer. He didn't have many close friends. Two exceptions were Pete Delaney and me. We used to spend many hours on the Presbyterian Church steps solving local, national and international problems.

Gary delivered papers after school. His territory delivering the *Knoxville News Sentinel* covered a large section of town. Gary prided himself on his ability to expedite his rounds by folding the paper into a small compact square. As a result, he was able to throw the paper from the street almost in front of the door. He preceded his toss by yelling, "pay-PAH!" as loud as he could. His customers were pleased with his delivery and announcement, but older folks sometimes had trouble unfolding the paper!

Gary was a year ahead of me in school. During his senior year, the school gave an I.Q. test for all the high school students. After notifying the students of the test results, they made a public announcement that Gary had scored the highest – over 150 – which as I understand put him in the genius class.

I think it was a mistake to do this because Gary stopped going to classes. He didn't do much homework anyway and would cram for the exams and still make a good grade.

Gary went off to college on a scholarship at Lincoln Memorial University in Harrogate, Tennessee. The school is not too far from Middlesboro, Kentucky. This is where one of my stories about Gary begins.

I was in my first year at the University of Cincinnati. I had attended Virginia Polytechnic Institute the previous two years. Gary was in his senior year at LMU.

I had called him the night before and told him I would be in Middlesboro late that afternoon to make connections for Cincinnati. That bus wouldn't be leaving until midnight, so we could spend a few hours together. It had been over two years since we had seen each other.

Gary was waiting for me when my bus arrived. After stowing my bag in a bus station locker, Gary took me to a fast food place for dinner. Then he suggested we go have ourselves a drink at the Middlesboro Hotel.

In Middlesboro at that time, you bought a bottle at the bar, then took it to a booth and ordered set ups – mixers that go with the booze. We bought a half pint of bourbon.

I had not known beforehand and Gary had not bothered to tell me that the Middlesboro Hotel was a whorehouse. It was a badly kept secret.

Gary had selected a high back booth in a far corner. I thought the reason was because it was quiet back there and very private.

Not too long after we poured ourselves a drink, an absolutely gorgeous woman plopped herself down very close to Gary and chastised him for not seeing her more often. She then proceeded to plant a big kiss on him and told him she had to go to do some business. I sat there speechless.

Let me back up here and explain something. Gary was not what you would call good looking. He wore thick glasses, was balding, and his figure might remind you of George Costanza of *Seinfeld* fame. Also, he was not known to be a ladies' man. Seeing me sitting there dumbfounded, he simply said, "I guess you figured it out that this is a whorehouse. Mary is the Queen Bee."

It didn't make sense! The absolute adoration she showed to Gary puzzled me. It would appear she could have any guy she wanted. Then Gary explained the whole story.

"As you know, I have always had odd jobs to make a little money. Thank God for the scholarship! You also know that I've never been successful around women. So when I got to LMU, I made up my mind to do something about it.

"I happened to wander into the Middlesboro Hotel lounge and night club. Like you, I did not know it was a whorehouse until a woman comes over and sits down beside me. 'Buy me a drink?' she asked. I had bought a half pint of bourbon, which took damn near all of my money.

"'I can't,' I quickly said and motioned for her to get out of the booth. I practically gulped down the bourbon because you can't take the bottle with you.

"Outside I was kicking myself for not coming up with a better answer. About a week later I came up with a plan. It would cost me a half pint a week, but I had to try it.

"On a weekday night I went into the hotel lounge and took a seat where you're sitting. In a short time, one of the women came over and started to sit beside me. I was sitting at the very edge of the seat so she could not sit beside me. I kept my head down and nursed my drink. She took a seat opposite me. She quietly asked, 'You wanna have a good time?' I didn't look up, shook my head 'no' and continued to stare at my drink.

"'You wanna talk?' she asked. Again I shook my head 'no.' She soon got up and left.

"Another woman came by. Standing beside me, she touched my shoulder and said she was available. I gave her the silent treatment too. She left in a huff. I finished my half pint and left.

"The next week I glanced into the lounge and found the back booth was empty. After buying a half pint I sat in the same place with my back towards the bar where the girls were sitting.

"Same thing happened as before. 'Hi,' she said, 'Weren't you in here last week?'

"I nodded my head 'yes' but I didn't say a word. 'Looking for some action?' she inquired. I didn't even look up and didn't say a word. She walked away.

"I hadn't quite finished my bottle when one of the women thought she would try her luck. She was very attractive. 'Mind if I sit down?' she asked. I just shrugged my shoulders. She started asking some questions, but I didn't answer. I took a big swallow of liquor abruptly got up and walked out.

"Three or four days passed before I ventured into the hotel again. The first thing I did was to see if the back booth was available. It was.

"Same scenario as before. Sip my whisky. Keep my head down. Back to the bar. Same old thing. The women would come up. The invitations were almost the same – maybe with a little variation.

"After doing this act for several weeks, I began to think it wasn't going to work. I kept telling myself, 'It's a good plan – just be patient.'

"Then it happened. Every one of the women had a go at trying to lure me into their bed. They surmised there must be something wrong with me. I could hear some of their mutterings. Then, finally – the Queen Bee herself came over to the booth! She had not visited me before. She probably knew through the other women that I likely didn't have any money since I only bought a half pint of bourbon, drank it and left the lounge. As you've seen, she's a real looker with a figure to die for… and she was the focus of my plan. I had to play this very carefully.

"Her opening line was 'What the hell's the matter with you? You come in here, buy a bottle and don't talk to nobody! You must know what this damn place is. So what is your problem? These girls have to have work!'

"I was trapped! My goal was to be laid by the prize whore without costing me a penny. Now she was challenging me to explain my behavior.

"'I, I, I, uh,' came out of my mouth while I groped for words. Then I said, 'I can't tell you.' And with that, I jumped up and left. Outside I was mad at myself because I left a partially drunk bottle on the table. But I did accomplish one thing. I met the star of the show!

"For the next week or so I pondered my next move that I should take. I thought, what the hell – I'll take it as it comes.

"For about the fifth or sixth time, I went in through the hotel lobby, checked the lounge and found my booth vacant. I couldn't have scripted it better.

"As soon as I sat down with my booze, she arrived and sat opposite of me just staring at me with those beautiful green eyes. Boy, was she my dream!

"'Last time I saw you, you said you couldn't tell me why you came in here and wouldn't talk to the girls!" she said, determined that she would get a reply. I affected a shutter, lowered my head, took a big swig straight from the bottle and, teary eyed, I said, 'My mother was a lady of the night!' I was so proud of my quick thinking, but I realized I probably would need more time for her to let this fact sink in so I quickly left.

"It was better than I thought it would be. So the next time when I went into the hotel, I sneaked a glance into the bar just to make sure she was there. She was.

"Not glancing right or left, I headed straight for the booth as I always had. Immediately, she came over and shoved me so she could sit beside me. She noticed that I had not bought a bottle so she gets up, goes to the bar and brings back a pint of bourbon and two glasses!

"After pouring two big slugs of the booze she held my hand. I faked crying. She softly said, 'I understand.'

"'I loved my mother so much!' I blubbered. 'She was so beautiful. Like you. Why my daddy left us, I'll never know. I was only eight or nine when she was in a car wreck and died. I was raised by my grandma. When I came to Middlesboro I happened to see you in here so I started coming in. You reminded me so much of my mom that I couldn't look at you! Instead I turned my back and just thought of you!

"I know I could have won an Academy Award! She was crying. She told the girls she was through for the night and took me to her home just outside of Middlesboro.

"We made love all night. And for free!"

Gary's Unionized Army

One of the U.S. Army's big mistakes was accepting Gary Collier when he was drafted and trying to turn him into a highly trained and disciplined soldier. Not that Gary wasn't patriotic; he just didn't accept authority too well.

He was also very a very diabolical sort. I think this story he once told me illustrates why I made it a point never to get Gary mad at me.

This story starts out in Honolulu, that tropical paradise. How Gary could get assigned to such a fantastic army post baffled my mind. Anyway, he was there as a Military Policeman. Talk about the fox guarding the chicken house! This gave him an opportunity to see firsthand the seedier side of paradise. His military duties took him to all the "off-limits" places were GIs were not to go. Somehow or another he blew this great assignment and landed on Johnson Island.

As I understand it, Johnson Island is a small, isolated, lonely strip of land in the Pacific, 800 miles southwest of Hawaii. It serves the United States military as a giant warehouse for war materials ranging from bulldozers to bandages.

Evidently, Gary had really done something wrong because the Army stripped him of all rank. He was a no-striper. His job was that of a stevedore; loading and unloading ships, storing material in huge bins – hard, manual labor in the tropical heat. You get the picture.

Needless to say, Gary was not happy about his fall from grace.

So what does Gary do? What any laborer would do if he was subject to those conditions – he forms a union!

A number of kindred souls found themselves in his same situation – GIs who had revolted against the system. According to Gary, it was like being in prison anyway. What more could they lose?

When you're secretly forming a union, what's the first thing you do? You file grievances. Gary found several. The Army officer in charge did not take too kindly to this challenge, so he refused to accept the complaints. Gary simply said he dismissed him.

So if they deny your complaints, what's the next thing a union man should do? Strike! And that's exactly what Gary and his fellow unionists did next.

As you can imagine, the officer-in-charge didn't appreciate one bit of this unusual form of insubordination. Gary simply said he was not used to dealing with unions.

And the results? Gary got what he wanted – he was discharged from the Army. I don't think he got a Dishonorable Discharge, but the next-to-dishonorable – called a "Less than Honorable Discharge" certificate. Gary didn't give a damn; he was out of the military… but not before he got his sweet revenge!

Sweet Revenge, Gary Style

As I mentioned before, Gary was diabolical. If he hated someone, he would find a way to get even. Such was the case of a Lieutenant Colonel on Johnson Island who was in charge of the stevedores. Gary, being the self-proclaimed union leader of his fellow stevedores and having his particular brand of difficulty with authority, was often at odds with this particular Lieutenant Colonel. None of the GIs objected to Gary's "title" and encouraged him to speak on their behalf.

While Gary was serving as a military policeman in Honolulu – before landing himself on Johnson Island – he had become well acquainted with the seedier section of the city. Somehow, despite his frequent violation of military protocol and many other infractions, he still was eligible to go on R&R (Rest and Relaxation). So, naturally, he high-tailed it to Honolulu.

His first stop was a well-known bar in that seedier part of town. There he ran into an old friend of his – a prostitute he had gotten to know earlier. Over drinks, she and Gary began commiserating about their respective problems – Gary's problem being the US Army and hers being the clap, which she had recently acquired.

Lo and behold, who should appear but the Colonel from Johnson Island – along with a couple of other officers who were stationed there with him. The bar was plenty crowded, so Gary and the girl managed to slip by without getting noticed by either the Colonel or his party. But they paused long enough for Gary to point out the Colonel to his friend.

Outside, Gary gave the prostitute a twenty with instructions for her to invite the Colonel for a "little bit of fun!" Naturally, she protested since she had VD, but Gary prevailed upon her to do this one thing just for him.

It worked. Because she was so attractive, the Colonel didn't hesitate to accommodate her.

Returning to Johnson Island, Gary had to be patient. The Colonel was at work every day and Gary began to doubt that his revenge had been consummated.

About a month passed when suddenly the Colonel disappeared from the Island. No one gave an explanation for his departure. Although, Gary heard through the grapevine the Colonel had "health problems"!

Dying Alone

In 1967 I was assigned to Wright-Patterson Air Force Base. Sonia and I bought a house in Fairborn, Ohio and settled down with our two children.

I had heard that Gary Collier was still in Cincinnati and had married a woman with a young son, owned a home and had become domesticated. Somehow I had difficulty believing that.

I called his home one evening and a woman answered. When I told her who I was, she said she was Gary's wife. Gary wasn't home and wasn't expected until very late, so I left a message for him to call me. Late in the afternoon the next day, Gary called.

It was like we had never been apart! We agreed to meet after work in a bar in the Western Hills section of Cincinnati.

I was excited to catch up with my old friend. After ordering drinks, we talked about what he was up to. He was an actuary for Hartford Insurance in downtown Cincinnati. He married late in life and he was fond of her son. She had a job (I can't recall what sort). Everything sounded like he may have changed his lifestyle.

I looked at my watch – after midnight! It was about an hour and a half drive from the bar to Fairborn so I said, "I've gotta go." I was so tempted to stay longer and shoot the breeze, but my sober side said I had better get home. A couple of drinks more would do me in. We planned to get together in the not too distant future.

When we met again, our plan was about the same except this time I would stay overnight at Gary's house. So I packed my pajamas and toothbrush.

Midnight came and went and Gary was still not ready to go home. I was getting plastered. Even though he lived close by, I was still concerned about driving while intoxicated. Gary assured me that there would be no problem. At 2:30 a.m. his wife would come and pick us up. I had forgotten that Gary never did learn how to drive! When I protested that I didn't want to have his wife get out of bed to come and pick us up, his answer shocked me. She did it all the time. It was automatic!

Without calling her, Gary's wife walked into the bar just as it was closing. That was the first time I had met her. She appeared to be in her early forties, pleasant looking and seemed to have a nice personality – despite the early hour and having just gotten out of bed!

She headed straight back to bed when we got into the house. I really felt sorry for her because she had to go to work the next morning. Then it dawned on me that Gary did too! So I said goodnight to her and Gary both and headed for the couch.

"Aren't you going to have anything to eat?" Gary asked. We had been drinking all evening and hadn't eaten anything. Suddenly I felt very hungry.

Gary grabbed me by the arm and led me into the kitchen. "Sit down!" he commanded. "I'll get the coals started."

He opens the refrigerator and takes out two sirloin steaks, two potatoes wrapped in foil and a head of lettuce. "What kind of salad dressing do you want?" he asked.

The table had been set. I was still dumbfounded at what was going on. "Look, Gary, it's three in the morning. You gotta get some sleep!"

"I'm not going in," he replied. "How do you like your steak? The coals are ready!"

I must admit the steaks were delicious! Every workday night Gary would drink until the bar closed, his wife would pick him up and take him home. In the refrigerator would be a steak, potatoes and a head of lettuce. Can you believe this routine?

I later learned that Gary missed work quite a bit because of his sleep pattern.

On the weekends he would play catch up by staying in bed. I felt so sorry for his longsuffering wife. But she loved him and continued to put up with his indecencies.

Another thing bothered me. He knew everyone in that bar. They greeted him with shouts of joy when he entered the saloon. "These are my really good friends!" he told me.

"Bullshit, Gary," I said "I've been here enough now to see that these are regulars. They are all glass clutchers – real hardcore drinkers. They really don't care about anyone but who's buying the next drink!"

This infuriated Gary. He didn't know what to say because he was so mad. I thought it best to leave and let him think about it. We didn't say goodbye.

Gary's wife called me crying. She said she could not take his behavior any longer. Could I help her?

Sonia and I invited Gary and his wife to our home for dinner. I suggested they arrive early so we could have a nice visit. What I really wanted to do was to buy some time.

I knew a psychiatrist who lived not too far away. On the phone I explained to him Gary's weird behavior. I also agreed to pay him for his time. We arranged for me to bring Gary to his home, which was also his office.

The Colliers arrived shortly after 4:00 p.m. on a Saturday afternoon. I asked Gary to go with me to talk to a guy I wanted him to meet. Upon arriving at this house, his PhD sign in the yard gave away my plan. Gary became upset. "Who is this guy?" he demanded.

As best I could I tried to explain that I wanted him to talk to my doctor friend because of his irregular sleeping habits. Reluctantly, Gary entered the house and I sat in the living room while the doctor and Gary talked.

About an hour later they came out. The ride to my house was very quiet. At last at dinner Gary began to chill out and we were able to have conversation. Immediately after dinner they left.

That evening I called the doctor. First thing he said was, "You realize that your friend is very bright, don't you?" I replied that I was well aware of that. "Simply speaking, he has a significant complex about being around people who he thinks are not as intelligent as he is," the psychiatrist explained. I had previously told the doctor about Gary's drinking and eating habits. "He drinks so he can numb himself and appear to be enjoying the people around him. He needs help. A lot of help!"

I thanked the psychiatrist. He told me there would be no charge, that he enjoyed meeting Gary who he too regarded as one of a kind!

About six months later, Gary's wife called me to tell me Gary had died of a massive heart attack. Forty-two years old! She also asked if I would be a pallbearer.

The day before his funeral, Sonia and I arrived early at the funeral home for his viewing. People trickled in. As we were introduced they all turned out to be friends of Gary's wife. I kept looking out for any of his "good friends" from the bar. I didn't recognize anyone.

Same story at the funeral. People from Hartford Insurance showed up. I think they came out of obligation more than friendship or respect.

I wondered – since he was absent from work so much, why didn't Hartford Insurance fire him? The answer is they wanted to but didn't. At the funeral I talked to a fellow employee who knew Gary well. He said Gary was the best actuary Hartford had and when he worked, he could turn out the figures.

Driving in the funeral procession, I broke down and cried uncontrollably. Through the tears, I told Sonia, "If I died and just a handful of people came to see me off, what a wasted life I'd have led!"

Part 5
Planting Roots in Fairborn, Ohio

Fairborn, Ohio is where Dad came to be an icon – a true pillar of the community since the Air Force brought him and his family there in July of 1967. Today, when I visit home, I can't walk more than fifty feet in a public place with my father without someone stopping us to say, "Hey, Joe! How's it going?"

But it isn't just that people know him. He knows them as well. Selling real estate in a town for over 30 years will do that, I suppose. But it also has a lot to do with Dad's infectious personality and notorious sense of humor.

Dad's seemingly encyclopedic memory of people and their histories has always amazed me. So I was shocked when he didn't recognize one of my Wright State professors on a recent visit. I thought perhaps his memory was starting to go. Then I realized he probably just didn't hear her name properly or recognize her because of her new hairstyle. Sure enough, when I prompted again, not only did he know her, he could tell you what house she bought and how much she paid for it in 1980.

Though my parents now technically live in Beavercreek, Ohio (the next town over), Fairborn is the place that holds their hearts. And it's the many people like my parents who make me proud to call Fairborn my hometown.

SOMAR Greeting Card Company

It was Sonia's idea and I thought it was great… great enough to invest $9,600 of our $15,000 severance pay from the Air Force.

The idea was simple enough. Manufacture a small, rectangular decal of an oval Christmas wreath with the center removed so the area would be open. Behind each decal, place your child's school photo and stick it to the inside of a card and SHAZAM! You have the beginnings of a do-it-yourself Christmas card. Joe Pettaluga, a designer and friend, drew the wreath and a stylish "Especially for you at Christmastime" with little holly leaves in green and red for the front of the card. The inside was blank so you could mount up to six "Foto-Frames" as we called them.

In March 1972, SOMAR Greeting Card Company (the largest greeting card company in Fairborn, Ohio) was born. I took Sonia's idea to the National School Studios in Jackson, Mississippi. They specialized in Elementary school kid photos. The year before in 1971 they had done 2.3 million elementary school kid's pictures!

They thought it was a great idea too and they could forecast many more pictures would be ordered as a result. Could I have a million photo frames ready by the end of July? You bet!

We worked out a deal where I would provide a package of ten cards, ten business size envelopes and 20 photo frames. I could hardly wait to get back to Fairborn to tell Sonia of our good fortune!

Do you know what a million of something looks like? I do now. A million photo frames filled our family room!

Sonia worked out a schedule. Since I was a morning person, I would get up, feed our two children breakfast and see them off to school. Then I would get to work packaging photo frames and Sonia would sleep in.

Sonia would get up later in the morning and during the day join me in packaging. After supper we would work on our project and she would stay up late working.

Towards the end of July we had completed our end of the agreement. Late in July we got a phone call from the president of National School Studios apologizing to us that the order was cancelled! Sonia and I were in a state of shock. How could they do this to us! What right did they have to renege? And what rights did we have to force them to keep their part of the bargain?

Unfortunately, we had no rights. We had nothing in writing. Our first business venture taught us there is no such thing as an oral contract.

Sonia tried to be optimistic. We contacted a mail order company and sold a few frames that way. We sold some to PTAs as fundraisers. Nothing caught on. To add insult to injury, the Internal Revenue Service taxed us on our inventory. To solve that problem I destroyed our inventory.

Then one fateful Saturday morning, I went to the bank to borrow money when I ran into Ken Durnbaugh…

Whadaya'Got to Lose?

It was in the fall of 1972 on a Saturday morning and I was coming out of the First National Bank in Fairborn, Ohio. In my hand was a deposit slip for $2,000 for our checking account. To get this I had to give the bank $3,600 worth of stock as collateral. The stock had been bought for my children's college fund. Now it was hocked because I was damn near broke.

Everything was going wrong in my life. SOMAR Greeting Card Company was defunct. My prospective job with the United States Information Service had been cancelled because Congress did not approve the funds. I had sent out 195 resumes for jobs throughout the U.S. and had replies from about 125 of them. After interviews I had four job offers, but I didn't want any of them. Here I was – 42 years old, almost broke, with a family to support and no prospects. It's safe to say that this was a real low point in my life.

My dear wife Sonia was doing her best to keep us functioning. Truly she was the tie that binds. I had to do something.

Walking out of the bank, I ran into Ken Durnbaugh. Ken and I were fraternity brothers at the University of Cincinnati. When he saw me he said, "Hi, Joe! What's the matter? I've never seen you looking so down!"

"Ken," I replied, "Everything I have done has turned into S-H-I-T!"

"Come on," he said. "Let's grab a cup of coffee."

"You buying?" I asked.

"Sure," he said.

Next door was the Colony Restaurant. There I poured out my miseries on Ken. He listened intently and said, "Why don't you sell real estate for me?" Ken was president of Art Homes, a large builder of homes in the area.

"Ken, don't think I'm an ingrate, but I can't see myself sitting in a new home all day. I'd go nuts!" I emphatically said.

"Then sell used homes," he said. "I own Fairborn Realty too."

"I dunno Ken," I said, downcast.

Ken leaned across the table and flatly said, "What the hell do you have to lose?" I'll make arrangements with my manager, Jim Lackey, for you to talk to him at ten o'clock Monday morning."

Ken was right. What did I have to lose? So I dressed in my best suit and tie and, arriving 15 minutes earlier than my appointment time, waited to talk to Mr. Lackey.

Mr. Lackey really didn't ask me many questions and within a very few minutes said, "You're hired!"

"What a dumb ass!" I thought. "He really didn't learn anything about me. I'll bet Ken Durnbaugh told him to hire me!"

I really dreaded taking the real estate exam. Even though I had taken the necessary courses at Sinclair College in Dayton, I was never thought of as a scholar by those who knew me.

In February 1973 I received the letter. I had passed!

Late in February I attended my first sales meeting. Jim Lackey went around the room asking the sales people what their goals were for the year. Shirley Hobby, the big gun at that time, announced that she was going to sell over $500,000 in properties. Everyone went "Ooh!"

When Jim came around to me he explained what the criteria were for setting goals. I told him I understood. "Shirley said she was going to sell $500,000. I'll sell $600,000!"

Everyone in the room went chuckle, chuckle, snort! New kid on the block! Even Jim Lackey laughed.

Maybe it was crazy for me to set such an audacious goal. But my experience in the Air Force had a lot to do with it. There you lived and died by your OERs – Officer's Effectiveness Reports – which were nothing more than the opinions of your superiors about your overall performance.

Now I had a chance to change all that. No longer would anyone else be able to write an OER on my performance – it would all be right out there in black and white. Either I made my goal or I didn't.

Thus began my real estate career. By the end of the year, I had met my goal – and then some. I had $932,000 in sales and was named Salesperson of the Year at Fairborn Realty. After 34 years in the business, there's not much more room on the wall for plaques and awards.

I guess the good thing about being at a low point is that it can be very motivating. There's no place to go but up.

Martin Cummins, the Steak Eater

In 1973, my first year in real estate, I was working with a young captain, Hugh Lynn, and his wife, Marigina. This was in the days when we Realtors qualified the buyers before we wrote an offer to purchase. We wanted to make sure the buyer had the wherewithal to buy the house.

I qualified Capt. Lynn for about $35,000. At that figure, I believed his payments would be pushing his comfort zone. I thought we had found the perfect house for him in the Forest Ridge area of Dayton. He and his wife felt the home was just great but too small. He wanted to look in Beavercreek.

With the exception of older homes in "old" Beavercreek, newer homes with the same square footage in the new plats were going for more than $35,000. But Capt. Lynn insisted we look in Beavercreek.

A brick two-story on a half acre lot in Sierra Park Estates caught his eye. A quick check of my MLS (Multiple Listing System) book showed it was newly built. The selling price was $50,000. The Lynns wanted to see it.

I put on my "Dutch uncle" hat to try to dissuade them from looking at it. "Capt. Lynn, you simply cannot afford it!" I said. But he insisted, so I drove to Jan Spencer Real Estate Office on Fairfield where I picked up the key to the house.

Even though the house was not quite finished, it still impressed Hugh and Marigina. They loved it! Hugh turned to me and said that he wanted to write an offer. I started to remind him that new homes normally sold for the asking price – no negotiations. Hugh accepted that. He then told me, "Joe, my dad has money and he told me, if we found something we liked, he would help my buy it." What a revelation!

It was about noon when I and the Lynns marched into Jan Spenser's office to write the offer to purchase. As it happened, the listing agent, Martin Cummins, and the builder both happened to be there too!

After writing the contract, we waited for the response which was immediately forthcoming. Signed, sealed and delivered! Boy was I elated! As a matter of fact, I was so elated that I offered to take everyone to lunch.

I even started to get greedy: Let's see – I was on a 50-50 commission. Fairborn Realty would get 50% of the commission and I would get 50% of that. The math was simple: 6% of $50,000 was $3000. Spencer Real Estate got $1500 and Fairborn Realty got $1500 – my half of that was $750. Wow! What a take home!

While I was grinning ear to ear, Martin Cummins walked up to me and mumbled something I could barely hear. I asked him to repeat it. In a muffled voice, he said, "Short commission."

"Short what?" I asked.

"Commission," he said a little louder. I could hardly believe what I was hearing.

"How much?" I asked in an irritated voice.

"$1500 total," he replied. "$750 to Fairborn and $750 to Spencer." I was beginning to feel sick. My sudden windfall had just fallen by half!

At the Melody restaurant, the waitress took our orders. That damn Martin Cummins ordered the biggest steak on the menu. I don't remember if I ate anything.

Through the years, I have told this story over and over again and the steak keeps getting bigger and bigger. Marty and I still go out to lunch at least once a week and he pays half the time. The experience was just a bad start to a great friendship.

The Million Dollar Club

Each year the Ohio Association of Realtors used to recognize agents who have sales of a million dollars or more. The criteria have changed over the years, but in the '70s it was based on the number of units (properties) sold or a total amount of your sales and listings. The contest began on the 1st of July and ended on the 30th of June the following year. One of my goals was to become a member of the Million Dollar Club. If you could achieve that for three consecutive years you were eligible to receive the Million Dollar Club Lifetime Membership. Only three or four real estate agents had achieved that goal at that time.

For two years I had been recognized for that achievement. The third year, I thought, would be a snap – that is until Friday, June 30, 1976.

I had three closings that fateful day. The first was scheduled for 9:30 a.m. in an attorney's office in Fairborn. I represented the seller who was selling his condo. Everything went smoothly. The seller received his proceeds check for over $30,000, part of which he was putting down to buy a house. That closing was supposed to happen at Citizen's Federal in downtown Dayton. Once again, everything went smoothly until the seller handed to the closing officer his check from the previous closing. The closing officer took the check and after examining it said, "We'll have to wait for three days to make sure this check clears."

Naturally, I hit the ceiling. "I cleared this with Bernice Moore who was scheduled to do the closing three days ago! She agreed to accept the check."

"Mrs. Moore is ill today, so I am doing the closing."

"I demand to see the president of Cit Fed now!" I shouted. I was able to see him, but he reminded me he had to support his closing officer and if we could wait a couple of days we could reschedule it.

I grabbed my buyer and said to the closing officer, we would get a cashiers check and be back as soon as we could. He agreed to keep the file open.

The seller said "What are we going to do now?" I told him we were going back to Fairborn and talk to the president of the First National Bank, Noah Lemaster. The seller asked me if I had collateral enough to cover the monies needed. I simply said no.

Fairborn is 14 miles from downtown Dayton. We made it back in about 20 minutes and walked into the bank. Dick Carnal was head of the loan department and his desk was near the front entrance. I walked straight up to him.

"Dick, I need $18,332.10 in a cashier's check," I flatly stated.

"Sure, Joe. What do you plan to use as collateral?" he asked.

"I can put up my house!"

"That's fine, but we'll need some time to get an appraisal and so forth," he explained.

"Dick, I need the money now!"

Just then Noah Lemaster came walking through the door. When I spotted him, I said. "Noah, do you want to hear a sad story?"

"Yeah, Joe, I haven't heard one all day!" he responded.

As quickly as I could I explained my problem. I had to complete all three closings that day to be eligible for the Million Dollar Club Lifetime Membership.

He listened intently and turning to Dick said, "Ok, he can borrow the money."

In a low whisper, Dick said, "He has no collateral."

Noah nodded his head and said, "I know."

Dick couldn't believe his ears. "What will he use as collateral?"

Noah asked, "Do you want me to write up the loan?"

"No, no, no," Dick said.

I almost kissed his ring finger!

In about 15 minutes I had a cashier's check made out to Citizen's Federal Savings and Loan. My buyer, a professor in finance at Wright-State University, couldn't' believe what happened. "Boy, you sure must have a good credit rating!"

"No," I replied, "just friends in high places!" The third closing went without a hitch.

Later that fall at the state convention, the certificates were handed out during a special luncheon.

When I returned home, I planned a party at the Rona Village Clubhouse. I sent invitations to all my customers who had made the achievement possible. I also invited certain others who went above and beyond and gave them special t-shirts. One went to Noah Lemaster. His read "Bank on Me!"

The party lasted until about three in the morning. I was one happy man.

The Roth Realty Christmas Party

The Roth Realty agents of Fairborn always put on the greatest parties at Christmastime. In addition to their customers, they invited other realtors.

At one of their parties, I was sitting on a desk in a salesperson's cubical. At the open end, a crowd had gathered to hear some of my corny jokes when the phone rang. After several rings someone called out "Joe, get the phone," so I did. However, unbeknownst to everyone else, the caller had hung up.

Seemed to me like a good opportunity to have some fun. I answered, "Roth Realty. How might I help you?" and then paused. "What priced home did you say you're looking for?" Again a pause. "How much money do you make a year?" Another pause. "Well, sir, we don't sell cheap houses to poor people!" and slammed down the phone.

Marion Watkins, the sales manager, damn near dove over the people to get at the phone. "What are you doing to us?" he exclaimed. "Gee, Marion, I thought this was a high-class outfit. Surely you would not deal with poor people or cheap houses!"

To this day I don't know if he believed me or not.

Joe Martin – Real Estate Agent, Client Rustler

Being a real estate agent is not as much fun as it used to be. Nowadays you have to be high tech because most of your customers are. You have many more rules and regulations than when I first entered the profession in the early '70s.

That was a kinder, gentler time when I could do some practical jokes. The one I liked most was when the F.J. Cooper Realty Company opened an office in Fairborn. It was located right beside Fairborn Realty where I was an agent. The buildings at that time were look-alikes – both Cape Cod designs with identical room layouts.

One evening I was sitting in my office with an Air Force major. We had just completed negotiations on a property in Beavercreek and had accepted a purchase contract.

I glanced through my window and saw a gathering of people in the "living room" of the office. It was nearing 7:30 p.m. and I thought to myself they must be having a sales meeting. I looked at the major and said, "I want you to do something for me."

"What's that?"

"I want you to go next door, walk in and announce I'm Major Smith and I'm looking for a home in the low 80s!"

"What are you going to do?" he asked.

"I'm coming in after you!" I replied.

"You're gonna get me killed," he said.

"No! No!" I said. "It will happen so fast they won't know how to react!"

He reluctantly agreed.

I waited outside just long enough for him to make his announcement. Tearing into their office, I said in a loud voice, "There you are! Get your ass back over to my office!" Which he did.

I no sooner got into my office when the phone started ringing. We had four lines and each one lit up. "You can't do that!" "I'll have your license!" "He's our client!" "You bring him right back!"

Even after I explained to several of their agents that they had been "had," old F.J. still wanted my license!

The Psychic

The Bible tells us that some people are "gifted," that is they can prophesy or speak in tongues, among other things. I had never witnessed a true psychic until I was in real estate.

I had "desk" duty, which required me to take phone calls and messages at the office for a certain number of hours, usually four.

A call came in and the lady wanted to see a listing our office had on a property in south Fairborn. I informed the lady that the house had been "propped," meaning the house had an accepted contract to purchase.

She said, "Are you refusing to show the house to me?"

"No, ma'am! I mean that it is sold and after the appraisal for the lender, a closing date will be set."

"I still want to see it."

"Okay," I replied. "I'll call the owner to set an appointment. When did you want to take a look?"

"Tomorrow after work. About five o'clock," she said.

"Alright, I'll call you back. Please give me your number," which she did.

The owner said, "I thought my house was sold. Why are you taking another person through? Is there a problem?" I tried to explain to him that because of her insistence she probably wanted to see the floor plan so if any other house like it came on the market she would have a good idea of what to expect. I went on to say that I could search the market for the same style of house if she did like it.

The seller was still dubious, but he agreed to the appointment time. I called her to confirm and she asked if I would meet her there and I agreed.

My manager had the property listed, so I thought it best to tell him about the showing. He said he had already gotten a call from the owner wanting to know if everything was going according to schedule and told him about my appointment. The manager assured the owner everything was okay, but he would talk to me. He then came to me and reiterated that the appraisal was done, no problems there, inspections were done, again no problems, and since he also had the buyers, they had been approved for the loan.

I met the lady at the appointed hour. She had a friend with her. The owner was not home, but I had a key to get in. The prospective "buyer" looked all around and didn't say a word until we were outside. She asked, "What do I do now?"

I was taken aback by her question. So I proceeded to tell her that we were pretty sure the buyers were going to close. "They're not going to buy the house!" she said very definitely.

"Do you know them?" I asked.

"No, I don't!" she said emphatically.

While I was trying to figure out if she knew something that I didn't know but was reluctant to tell me, her friend came closer to me and whispered in my ear, "She sees things!"

"You understand if we write a contract to buy the house it would be what we call a 'backup' contract that only gets invoked in the event the other offer falls through." I emphasized this point as best I could. She nodded her head that she understood.

She and her friend drove to my office and, after locking up the house, I went directly to meet them. I prepared the contract and asked her what she wanted to offer. "What are they asking?" she asked. I told her. "Well, that's what I want to offer." She replied.

In reality the other offer was for full price also, but I had not told her that. A clean contract, full price, no inspections other than termite and she wrote an earnest money check. And again, I emphasized that this was a "backup" contract.

She did, however, want her husband to approve of the purchase. He was a long-distance truck driver and would not be back until Thursday afternoon. No problem, I assured her.

After the ladies left, I called my manager. "You really wrote a contract? You're sure she doesn't know something that we don't know?"

The next morning the manager called the seller and told him about the offer. He assured the seller who was getting really nervous about all this that the buyer had qualified for the loan and we were waiting for the mortgage company to give the okay to set a time and date with a title company to do the closing.

No sooner had he hung up the phone when another call came in. It was the manager's original buyer.

"Is it possible to get out of my contract?" he asked. He explained that he had just gotten a call from his mother that his father had a heart attack and could he come to Germany right away and take over his father's business, which was a shoe store. This all happened on Tuesday morning.

The manager went into a state of shock. "You didn't know it, but we have just presented a backup contract to the owner, which he accepted. The only stipulation was that her husband who is out of town has to approve the purchase. He will be in Thursday. So, yes, you have a very good chance of getting out of the contract and getting your money back!"

The manager called me with the news. "You're not going to believe this!" and went on to tell me about his conversation with his buyer. I, in turn, called my psychic and relayed the good news. She was not surprised, but reminded me that her husband was the final authority.

Thursday, late in the afternoon, I accompanied the psychic and her husband through the house. walked outside and said, "Honey, I love it. You did a great job in finding it!"

Naturally, I was elated. Her prediction had come through! "What do we do now?" he wanted to know.

"We'll go back to the office and strike out the contingency that you have to approve the contract and we're set to go."

Back at the office I was ready to strike the contingency when she said, "Don't sign that!"

I could scarce believe what I just heard. "Why *not*?"

"I'd rather not talk about it," she calmly replied.

Her husband turned to her and said, "What's the matter, honey? Are you seeing something?" He then turned to me and explained, "She sees things!"

"Yeah, I'm beginning to see that."

Once again her reply was, "I'd rather not say!"

"Look, honey," he said, "you're driving this man crazy! You gotta tell him something! You know I'm leaving tomorrow at 6:30 in the morning, so we've got to get this straightened out tonight!"

In a very definite voice she said, "You're going to go on strike!"

"Now, now, honey! When I came in today, they had that problem all solved. There's not gonna be a strike!" he said.

"Yes, there is," she calmly said.

Her husband looked at me and said, "Now what do we do?"

"Well," I said groping for words. "I guess you can put your initials on the contingency. If you go on strike, call me first thing in the morning when you get to work and let me know. If you are, I'll leave the contingency as it is – there is no contract unless it's removed." I called my manager with the bad news that his original buyer had been released from the contract.

At six o'clock the following morning, my phone rang. It was the psychic's husband. "You're not going to believe this. We are on strike! I can't even get into the depot because the gates are locked! They had a wildcat strike last night and the bosses shut the place down. I'm calling you from a pay phone!"

"Thanks for calling," I managed to utter. What on earth am I going to do now? Both buyers are out of the contract and the sellers are going to go ballistic. As I pondered, the ringing phone jarred me. It was her!

"Don't worry," she cheerfully said. "The people who wanted the house in the first place will buy it. So don't worry!"

"Yeah, sure!" I managed to say and I didn't want to talk anymore about it. I was sick!

The manager called me about eight that morning and said that he had just gotten a call from his buyers asking if there was any chance of getting their contract back on the house! I informed him about my conversations earlier that morning and told him everything was back in his hands.

I never attempted to contact that lady again, nor did she ever call me. I scratched out her name from my prospects list.

The night I showed her the house, her friend told me about her visions. While she looked through the house her friend elaborated. She sees all kinds of things, like car wrecks, fires, airplane crashes, and it frustrates her so much because she doesn't know the people or who to contact so she can warn them.

I can believe that. I don't want to work with anyone "who sees things!"

I Sure Hope They Have a Dog!

Back in our Dynamic Duo days, when my partner, Palmer Bolling (more about him later), and I would go out on a listing appointment together, I would have done the research and prepared the paperwork beforehand and would then make the presentation. Then Palmer and I would go through the property and I would make notes from my own observations along with Palmer's and the owner's statements.

After the tour, we would sit down, preferably at a kitchen table, with the sellers and discuss marketing, comparable properties that had sold, financial considerations (current interest rates, for example) and general observations. After all that, we would go back to the office and I would prepare the final presentation. A two-step process. At our next meeting, after discussing the pros and cons of the property, I would announce our findings or suggestion of market value. Palmer would observe the reaction of the sellers.

On one such occasion, we returned for our second meeting. After everyone was comfortably seated, I began explaining the procedures for determining value. The house was a large, brick two-story on five acres of farmland and pasture – a very nice home.

I had prepared a paper with our suggested asking price. As I was handing the paper to the man of the house, I said, "I believe the value to be $175,000." Upon hearing that, the owner pushed my hand away. He muttered something I didn't quite hear.

Palmer had quickly gotten up from the table. Dumb me, I asked if the owners had any questions. Finally, it dawned on me that I had really made the seller mad, so I quickly crammed all my paperwork into my briefcase. The owner ushered us out the front door.

Lying there across the threshold of the open door was an old hound dog. The owner kicked the dog, which quickly retreated, howling all the way. Palmer looked over at me and we both scurried out of the house and into my car.

From that day on Palmer paid closer attention to the owners during my listing presentation. If he sensed something, he would whisper, "I sure hope to hell they have a dog!"

El Burpo's

A Lieutenant Colonel stationed at Wright Patterson Air Force Base was nearing retirement. He thought he would never be transferred to a new base, but he was.

His problem was that he owned a small Mexican restaurant located in Fairborn, near WPAFB, catty-cornered from our Hearth real estate office. He didn't want to be an absentee owner, so he came to talk to my partner Palmer and me about selling the place.

To digress slightly, when I was stationed at Holloman AFB in New Mexico, Sonia and I would drive about 70 miles to eat at a famous Mexican restaurant, La Posta, in Old Mesilla, near Las Cruces. In our opinion, the best Mexican food we ever tasted was in New Mexico, not Mexico! I believe that was for two reasons. The first was the cooking, influenced by the highly civilized Navajo Indians and secondly, the peppers, grown in Hatch, New Mexico.

When the Lt. Col. talked to us about marketing his restaurant, he turned to me and said, "Joe, you're always eating at my restaurant. How about buying it!"

I looked over at Palmer to see his reaction and could tell he wasn't impressed with the idea. But I was.

"How much are you asking, Colonel?"

"What do you think it's worth?"

Even though we had reviewed his financial statement, I could not come up with a value. That didn't stop me from blurting out, "Fifty thousand dollars!"

He thought for a moment and said he would take no less than $60,000, which would include the fixtures and inventory.

"Would you be willing to sell it to us on a land contract?"

"At what interest rate?"

I thought for a moment and said, "Six percent."

He almost jumped out of his seat. "You know what interest rates are today?"

"Sure," I replied. But that's the deal."

The colonel took it.

Palmer was still not sure about the whole idea but liked the terms. I assured him that I would monitor the running of the restaurant and Palmer knew a restaurant owner, Phil Neibert, who agreed to manage the place.

In about a month, we were in business. We spent about $10,000 renovating the interior. We even changed the name to La Casita – the little house.

Sonia had a recipe book from the fabulous La Posta and Phil calculated recipes from it for increased amounts of food.

We started making a few bucks. The personnel turnover was something else. Phil decided to pay more attention to the restaurant he owned. A lady who began working with us when we bought the place became our head waitress.

Because our real estate office was so near, I would drop in every day to see how things were going. Our business was so-so. There was a succession of cooks. I don't think some of them could even read the recipes!

For example, one day I went in for lunch and couldn't believe how bad the salsa tasted. I went stomping into the kitchen.

"Who made this salsa?"

"I did," replied the head cook.

"Didn't you taste it?" I asked.

"I don't eat that shit," he answered unapologetically.

Naturally, we let him go.

La Casita continued to flounder until one day a handsome man whom we will call Jefferson Blacksocks, applied for the head cook's job. A Navajo from New Mexico who loved to cook!

At the same time, we hired a pretty blonde as hostess. She had attended Antioch College and said she "just loved working in quaint places." You know the type.

Business grew and pretty soon customers would angrily tell me, "I couldn't find a parking place!" You're gonna have to do something about that."

"Thank you, Lord," I thought.

Everything was going just fine until one night one of our waitresses returned to La Casita after it closed to pick up something she had forgotten. She had the key because she was scheduled to open up the following day.

We had closed at 9 p.m. and it was after 10 o'clock when she walked into the kitchen. This is the way she described what she saw.

"Right there on the food preparation table was Jefferson and That Woman!" (Our waitresses never really cared for our hostess and often referred to her as "That Woman.")

Well, all the waitresses were in revolt. I suggested getting rid of the hostess. No, that wasn't good enough. I had to fire Jefferson, too.

We were doing so well and now this! After the two lovers left, we were back to the old problem: cooks who didn't appreciate Mexican food. If only we hadn't hired That Woman!

Palmer and I sold the place shortly after that. We actually made a few bucks on the sale but were left with a wardrobe deficit. All of our ties had salsa splatters on them!

No, I Don't Want to Own a Real Estate Company

Bad news. Ken Durnbaugh announced he was selling Fairborn Realty to one of his company's officers. This was in 1976 and I had been selling real estate for three years.

After evidently dismissing Jim Lackey, the new owner offered me the manager's job.

I was in a quandary. I loved selling real estate, but I certainly did not want to manage an office.

Now I need to pause for a minute here and tell you about how I met Palmer Bolling. Palmer worked for Ken Durnbaugh in his new house sales division. The first time I met him, I noted his accent. It definitely was from the hills.

"Where are you from?" I asked.

"You wouldn't know it," he replied. "It's a little place called Pound in the Southwest corner of Virginia."

"Sure! That's where I first tasted mutton on Owen Bolling's farm!"

"He's my great uncle!" he practically shouted.

"Hi, cuz," I said laughing at the prospect.

Palmer did not know much about appraising properties; he was always too busy selling them and spent most of his time stuck in a new home or condo holding an open house. So he and I struck up a deal. He would refer people to me when they wanted to buy an existing home and we would split the listing. This arrangement was working out well.

So when Ken announced the buyout of Fairborn Realty, Palmer started into bugging me. "Why don't we open our own real estate office?"

"Hell, no!" was my often response. "I just want to sell real estate and I don't want the responsibility of managing an office or agents."

"I'll manage the office," said Palmer, "and I'll manage the sales agents, too! Now why don't we open our own office?"

Soon it became apparent that I was going to have to make a decision. But one thing still bothered me – you have to be a broker to own a real estate office and neither Palmer nor I were brokers. Palmer soon called me with a solution: Jim Lackey had a broker's license and was now without a job. Jim told Palmer he would be happy to be a part owner of a company and volunteered to be sales manager.

Palmer made his final appeal: "Now what's it gonna take for you to join Jim Lackey and me and own our own company?"

I boldly stated my three conditions:

1. My own office;

2. Everything split evenly;

3. Nothing to do with sales people.

"Deal!" said Palmer and Jim.

And now for the name. How do you choose a name? Palmer, Jim and I sat in a bar at the Holiday Inn in Fairborn trying to come up with a name. Suddenly I realized it was 11:00 p.m. "I'd better call Sonia." When I told her what we were trying to do, she suggested "Hearth" – it connotes a feeling of hominess and warmth. We eventually adopted the slogan "Hearth and Home Inseparable." Joe Pittaluga, an old Air Force buddy, designed a simple logo for us with an orange flame, dark brown lettering and a beige background.

Hurriedly we rented a building next to Fairborn Realty and filled it with card tables and folding chairs. Within two weeks, we were in business.

I won't go into details, but Palmer and I didn't like Jim Lackey's style of management and we eventually decided we would try to buy him out. But we sill had the same problem as before – neither Palmer nor I were brokers.

It was almost like God answered our prayers when Jim announced that Ken Durnbaugh offered him the job of sales manager of Omnico (formerly Art Homes). He agreed to give us time to schedule a broker's exam. Fortunately, the following week we found an opening for the test in Columbus.

Armed with all kinds of books on real estate practices and procedures, appraising, financing and the like, we booked a hotel room in Columbus the day before the test and crammed as much as we could. The broker's exam was much harder than the agent's exam. We figured if just one of us passed we would be in business. Thank the Lord we both passed!

From the start, we had our eye on a closed-down Shell Service Station, which sat on the corner of Broad and Main in Fairborn. What an ideal spot! Shortly after we started Hearth, we bought the property and began the costly expense of remodeling.

Palmer took over as Principal Broker and sales manager. I didn't feel it was right for him to have all the responsibility without additional compensation, so we agreed to a 10% override on the salesperson's commission. I was happy and he was too.

We must have been doing something right because over the years – despite ups and downs in the real estate market, Hearth Realty grew. It wasn't too many years until we outgrew our office building and had to build an addition and then a second story just a year later. In 1981, we built a brand new second office in Beavercreek – an area we saw was primed for growth. At its peak, Hearth had over 70 agents with offices in Fairborn, Beavercreek, Xenia and Jamestown. By just about any measure, we were the largest real estate agency in all of Greene County, which was really saying something as the national franchises started moving in.

Sadly, Palmer died in 1997 at the age of 66. He had been an accounting and finance officer in the Air Force. With his mother's help in fibbing about his age, he enlisted at the ripe old age of 16 and retired as a major – an old man of 36! He's a classic example of a person with smarts who can advance in the Air Force. He was one of a kind and I am the luckiest man on earth to have had him as a partner.

After Palmer died I reluctantly became president and principal broker of Hearth. I made a couple of changes here and there to put my own personal stamp on the company, but mostly I just let things be. Palmer had run an effective organization and I didn't want to mess it up too much. I kept the company until February 2003 when I sold the company to a group of Hearth agents who later sold it to Coldwell Banker Heritage Realtors. In 2004, I sold Hearth's original Fairborn office building to a law firm. We worked it out so I could keep my old office for as long as I'm kicking around.

As of this writing, I'm an agent for Coldwell Banker, Dayton's largest real estate company. My partner for the last six years, Bill Richards, is a retired Chief Master Sergeant. He's a great guy and likes taking care of some of the things I don't like to do as much. I work most every day, but I don't have to run the show. I've got the flexibility to travel with Sonia and stay active in our community.

Things are pretty much how I like them. I guess there are things I would maybe do a little differently here and there, but as I reflect on all these stories and the memories that go with them, I reckon that a man couldn't ask for much more from this world.